▊fastread

BUYING AND LEASING A CAR

All the steps you need to know to get the car you want

Adams Media Corporation

Avon, Massachusetts

EDITORIAL

Publishing Director: Gary M. Krebs

Managing Editor: Kate McBride

Copy Chief: Laura MacLaughlin

Acquisitions Editor: Jill Alexander

Development Editor: Michael Paydos

PRODUCTION

Production Director: Susan Beale

Production Manager: Michelle Roy Kelly

Series Designer: Daria Perreault

Cover Design: Paul Beatrice and Frank Rivera

Layout and Graphics: Brooke Camfield, Colleen Cunningham, Michelle Roy Kelly, Daria Perreault

Published by
Adams Media Corporation
57 Littlefield Street, Avon, MA 02322. U.S.A.
www.adamsmedia.com

ISBN: 1-58062-696-3

Printed in Canada

J I H G F E D C B A

Library of Congress Cataloging-in-Publication Data
available from the publisher.

This publication is designed to provide accurate and authoritative information with regard to the subject matter covered. It is sold with the understanding that the publisher is not engaged in rendering legal, accounting, or other professional advice. If legal advice or other expert assistance is required, the services of a competent professional person should be sought.

> —From a *Declaration of Principles* jointly adopted
> by a Committee of the American Bar Association
> and a Committee of Publishers and Associations

Many of the designations used by manufacturers and sellers to distinguish their products are claimed as trademarks. Where those designations appear in this book and Adams Media was aware of a trademark claim, the designations have been printed in initial capital letters.

This book is available at quantity discounts for bulk purchases.
For information, call 1-800-872-5627

contents

introduction

Buying or leasing a car—especially a new car—is an exciting time. From hundreds of models, dozens of colors, and a vast array of options and add-ons, you get to select a car that suits your lifestyle and matches your tastes. You may imagine yourself purchasing a hunter green convertible with tan leather interior and driving with the top down, the wind in your hair. (Wait a minute—that's my fantasy, not yours!) Perhaps you pour over brochures, wade through information on Web sites, or work through classified ads to find your perfect match. You may make a list of the cars you want to test-drive.

But this all happens before you approach a dealership or talk to an individual who's selling a used car. The moment you exit the world of catalogs and Web pages and enter a dealership, reality sets in. You'll have to stick to a budget, find out which cars last the longest, choose a practical vehicle, compare fuel efficiency, meet salespeople, negotiate a price, perhaps forgo the add-ons and extras, decide whether to buy or lease, finance your purchase, and sign piles of paperwork. Welcome to the brave new world of buying or leasing a car. Between you and the new sports car you have your eye on is a whole bunch of hassles.

But you've come to the right place. *fastread*® *Buying and Leasing a Car* will quickly help you choose the right vehicle. Do you want to go with a new car or one that's gently used? Is it best to lease or purchase? What extras and add-ons do you need? This book will help you decide.

You'll also find out how much cars cost the dealers and how much they're really worth, how to avoid lemons, and how to negotiate the best price, finance the deal, and maintain your car's resale value. You get the lowdown on finding the right car at the best price in plain English. You also get some fun chapters that tell you about great Web sites, magazines, car shows, and automotive events around the country. You even get translations from carspeak into words you use every day so that you won't confuse a finance charge with a destination charge.

In short, reading this book before you set foot onto a dealer's lot or call about a used car will save you time, money, and plenty of aggravation.

chapter one

Selecting the Right Type of Vehicle for You

Before you visit showrooms, test-drive vehicles, or negotiate prices, you want to narrow your list of potential vehicles that
will meet your needs. Ideally, you want your list to include only
one or two makes (that's the manufacturer of the vehicle, like
Ford or Honda) and two to four models (that's the name of the
vehicle, like a Focus or an Accord). In order to choose from
among the hundreds of new vehicles—and thousands of used
ones—available, start by deciding which category of vehicle
you're most interested in.

For the most part, you can break vehicles down into basic
categories. Most people, for example, can picture what a car in the
"station wagon" category or the "sports car" category looks
like—they are similar in size, appearance, or features. Each manufacturer makes its cars look a little different and have unique features, though, so within each of these categories, you still have

lots of models to choose from.

This chapter helps you work through your overwhelming number of options so that you don't have to look at all kinds of cars before you find the one you'd like to buy or lease.

Sedans

Most cars on the road are sedans: These are cars with a trunk, two or four doors, and seating for four or five people. (When you think "car," a sedan is usually the first thing that comes to mind.) Sedans are practical and often quite comfortable to drive and ride in. The price range runs the gamut: Some sell for as low as $15,000, while luxury sedans can cost over $50,000 (see the "Luxury Cars" section, later in this chapter). And of course, your options are vast.

Sedans tend to get average to poor gas mileage, depending on their weight. Higher-priced sedans do well in crash tests, as do some of the lower-priced sedans. Consider the following highly rated sedans:

- Acura 3.2TL
- Buick LeSabre
- Chevrolet Malibu
- Dodge Intrepid
- Honda Accord
- Mitsubishi Galant
- Nissan Maxima
- Toyota Avalon
- Toyota Camry
- Volkswagen Jetta
- Volkswagen Passat

Compact Cars

Compact cars are true to their names—they're not quite as tiny as a breadbox, but they sure are small. Most compact cars have a hatchback (although some are compact sedans, and have trunks instead), are fairly low to the ground, and fit into small parking spots. Their main attraction is that they are among the lowest-priced vehicles you can buy and get decent gas mileage, so you save money all around. Tall people may find compact cars extremely uncomfortable, and nearly everyone will feel stiff and sore after a long trip in a compact car. Even on shorter trips, four people is about all that most compact cars can comfortably hold.

Also, compact cars often score low in crash tests, especially when struck by a heavy vehicle, like an SUV or a semi-truck. For this reason, before purchasing a compact car, carefully check its safety rating (see Chapter 2 for tips on how to find this information).

If you're interested in this vehicle category, take a look at the following models:

- Ford Focus
- Honda Civic
- Hyundai Elantra
- Mazda Protegé
- Mitsubishi Lancer
- Nissan Sentra
- Saturn SL
- Toyota Corolla
- Toyota Echo
- Volkswagen Golf
- Volkswagen New Beetle

Sports Cars

Sports cars are fun, fast, and attractive, and are popular among teenage drivers, anyone going through a midlife crisis, and genuinely cool people. They generally have two doors and either a hatchback or a trunk. Many come equipped with sunroofs (often called moonroofs), while others are convertibles.

In general, sports cars get poor to average gas mileage, score average in crash tests, and can't comfortably fit more than four (and in some cases, two) people. But you don't buy a sports car because of gas mileage or safety features, and you certainly don't buy a sports car to haul your family around—you buy a sports car because it looks so darned beautiful and drives so darned fast. And that beauty and speed comes at a price: Sports cars tend to be expensive. Because a sports car should be fun to drive, consider getting one with a manual transmission (stick shift).

If you want to increase your hipness quotient, consider buying or leasing the following:

- Audi TT Roadster
- BMW 3-Series
- Chevrolet Camaro Z28
- Chevrolet Corvette
- Ford Mustang
- Honda Prelude
- Honda S2000
- Mazda MX-5 Miata
- Mercury Cougar
- Mitsubishi Eclipse
- Toyota Solara

Keep in mind that people driving red cars tend to get more tickets than those in more subtly colored vehicles, so you may, instead, want to opt for British racing green. Also remember that sports cars tend to be expensive to insure, perhaps because some can travel at over 100 miles per hour with the same comfort that a sedan traveling at 50 miles per hour offers.

Station Wagons

Station wagons are the exact opposite of sports cars: They fit a lot of people, haul a lot of stuff, are built like tanks (and, thus, do pretty well in crash tests and tend to last for years and years), and are fairly inexpensive to insure.

Of course, all that efficiency and safety comes at a price: With a station wagon parked in your driveway, you'll be a permanent resident of Dullsville. Not once during the entire time you own or lease a station wagon will anyone say, "Cool car" or, "Can I take it for a spin?" or, "I've been thinking of test-driving one of those." They will, however, say things like, "I think you should drive the Girl Scout troop this Saturday—after all, you do have that station wagon."

So if you're extremely self-confident and can brush off the snickering at your next high school reunion, get yourself a station wagon. If not, consider a minivan (see the following section), which has many of the same features without the pocket protector status.

If you're interested in this vehicle category, take a look at the following models:

- BMW 5-Series Sport Wagons
- Ford Focus
- Hyundai Elantra
- Mercedes-Benz E-320
- Subaru Legacy
- Volkswagen Passat
- Volvo V40

Minivans

The arrival of the minivan nearly twenty years ago brought joy to the hearts of station wagon drivers who wanted to ride around in something a little more attractive. Minivans offer plenty of room for cargo and passengers (sometimes up to eight or nine) and tend to do well in crash tests. The main disadvantage of minivans, however, is that they generally get low gas mileage and are fairly expensive to buy—and they announce to the world that you've officially grown up and joined the ranks of the middle-aged.

Minivans are becoming much more flexible than they used to be. Many now have removable seats that allow you to haul an object as large as a sofa inside your vehicle. Some even come with electric doors, or doors on both sides of the vehicle, making entry and exit easier.

Consider these most popular minivans:

- Chevrolet Venture
- Chrysler Town and Country
- Dodge Grand Caravan
- Ford Windstar
- Honda Odyssey
- Plymouth Voyager
- Toyota Sienna

Sport Utility Vehicles (SUVs)

Sport utility vehicles—commonly referred to as SUVs—are similar to minivans, but driving an SUV projects a totally different image. Because most are equipped with four-wheel drive, the first SUV drivers were people who read *Outside* magazine: rugged hikers and mountain bikers who needed to lug sports equipment and camping gear down rutty dirt roads without getting stuck in the mud. Before long, however, people whose idea of exercise is walking to the mailbox began driving to work in SUVs, and the popularity of these vehicles soared. (Less than five percent of SUV owners actually take their vehicles off-road!)

Although they usually have less interior room than minivans, SUVs can still haul plenty of cargo and passengers and have excellent towing capabilities. They tend to do well in crash tests—mostly because of their sheer weight—but this feature also gives them lousy gas mileage. In fact, SUVs have recently come under fire for being environmentally unfriendly.

And because many SUVs sit so high off the ground, they are less stable than other vehicles and are more likely to roll over. Their least attractive feature? The price. SUVs are quite expensive, both to purchase and insure.

Models in this fast-growing category are almost too numerous to mention, but the following are the front runners:

- Chevrolet Suburban/ GMC Yukon XL
- Chevrolet Tahoe/ GMC Yukon
- Ford Escape/ Mazda Tribute
- Ford Explorer
- Jeep Grand Cherokee
- Jeep Wrangler
- Toyota Land Cruiser
- Toyota 4Runner

You can also find an emerging new type of SUV—one that combines an SUV with a station wagon—that's commonly called a soft roader. They look like shorter, longer versions of SUVs, but with all the SUV advantages. The Volvo Cross Country and Subaru Outback are classic examples of this new SUV design. Toyota's newest car, called Matrix, fits loosely into the SUV/station wagon category, although Matrix looks more like a compact car than a station wagon. Still, it offers four-wheel drive, has plenty of cargo space, and seats five.

Mini-SUVs

If an SUV is out of your price range and you're uncomfortable with poor fuel efficiency, consider a mini-SUV—a smaller, lighter, cuter version of the original. Mini-SUVs, commonly referred to as "cute-utes" and "sport-cutes," have several attractive features: Most have four-wheel drive, get decent gas mileage, cost just a few thousand dollars more than a sedan with similar features, and still allow you to haul a lot of cargo. Most mini-SUVs also comfortably fit five passengers.

If you're interested in this increasingly popular vehicle category, check out the following models:

- Honda CR-V
- Isuzu Amigo
- Kia Sportage
- Nissan Xterra

- Subaru Forester
- Suzuki Grand Vitara
- Toyota RAV4

Pickup Trucks

Pickup trucks are all about hauling stuff, although the most expensive models also offer comfortable interiors. One of the most attractive features of trucks, though, is that they're inexpensive: You can get a basic truck for about $13,000, but at that price, your vehicle isn't going to be very comfortable on a long trip (although the furniture you're hauling will be!).

Trucks get average gas mileage—better than SUVs and minivans, anyway—but can't comfortably seat many people. Even with an extended cab (which usually has an extra bench seat or small jump seats that fold out from the wall of the truck), the one or two people in the back won't be comfortable enough to take a long trip with you. If you buy a truck with automatic transmission and you really squeeze in, you might be able to fit three people in the front seat. With a manual transmission, though, your front-seat limit is two people. If you do opt for an extended cab, consider a truck that has one or two separate doors for the back seat—even if you don't plan to have people ride back there, getting your gear into the back will be much easier with a separate door. This is, however, a fairly expensive option.

Most pickup trucks are lightweight vehicles equipped with front-wheel drive, so they can be difficult to drive in snow. (If you live in a snowy climate, consider a truck with four-wheel drive, which is also a pricey option.) Also, because of their height-to-weight ratio, light pickup trucks do poorly in crash tests.

The major disadvantage of pickup trucks, though, is that you'll frequently be asked to haul other people's stuff whenever they move, buy a new washer, take a sofa in for reupholstering, and so on. Your best bet is to get into the habit of lending your truck (and using the borrower's car) so that you don't throw out your back helping all your friends, family, and neighbors move. (Be sure to check with your insurance agent about coverage during the loan of your truck.)

Also, if you'll be using your truck for hauling (and, really, what other reason is there to purchase one?), invest in a bedliner, which is a plastic shell or painted-on coating that keeps the metal bed underneath from scratching. They don't cost much and will keep your truck bed from rusting.

If you're interested in a pickup truck, take a look at the following models:

- Chevrolet Silverado/ GMC Sierra
- Dodge Dakota
- Dodge Ram
- Ford F-Series

- Ford Ranger
- Mazda B-Series
- Nissan Frontier
- Toyota Tacoma
- Toyota Tundra

Combination SUVs and Pickup Trucks

This category is brand-new and could well end up being quite popular. Combination vehicles have a front end like an SUV and a back end that looks like a small truck bed. These vehicles can't carry quite as many people as an SUV can or haul quite as much cargo as a pickup truck does, but the combination of the two vehicle categories gives you a lot of flexibility. The passenger part of combination vehicles provides a smooth and comfortable ride, while the truck bed is available for hauling large and awkwardly shaped objects.

You won't find many players in this category just yet: Look for the Chevrolet Avalanche, Ford Explorer Sport Trac, and Cadillac Escalade. They're all still fairly expensive and get low gas mileage, but both features will likely improve before long.

These new combo vehicles don't have a set name as of yet. So far, SUT (sport utility truck) and SUP (sport utility pickup) have been the most frequently used terms, And Chevrolet is trying to coin its own new term for these vehicles: the UUV (ultimate utility vehicle).

Hybrids

Most vehicle categories are based on the size or appearance of the vehicle: Compact cars are small, SUVs are large, sports cars are attractive, and so on. However, the common feature among hybrids is fuel efficiency.

Hybrids rely on two power sources—gasoline and electric power, and this allows them to have a small, efficient gasoline engine that can squeeze nearly sixty miles out of every gallon of gas. Unlike electric cars that were gaining popularity back in the 1980s, you don't have to plug in these cars to recharge them. Instead, a set of batteries (that supply power to the electric motor) recharge when the gasoline engine is running. Also unlike electric cars, hybrids don't struggle to go uphill or have limited ranges in which they can travel: When the car is going up a hill, the electric motor assists, using energy from the batteries, and when the car goes downhill, the batteries are recharged. As the batteries discharge, the gasoline engine takes over until the batteries are ready to supply power to the electric motor again, so you can take your hybrid as far as you'd like—even on a trip across the country.

Hybrids tend to be on the small side—Honda has a two-seater, and Toyota has a small sedan that's about the size of a Toyota Corolla. They also cost more than comparably sized, gasoline-only vehicles: The Honda Insight retails for $19,420, while the Toyota Prius starts at $20,480. However, you get a generous warranty with each: eight years/80,000 miles on the Insight's powertrain and batteries, and three years/36,000 miles on everything else; eight years/100,000 miles on the Prius's batteries and hybrid system, and three years/36,000 miles on everything else. And the gas mileage is phenomenal: The tiny Insight gets 60 miles per gallon (mpg) in the city and 68 mpg on the highway, while the larger Prius gets 52 mpg in the city and 45 mpg on the highway (that's not a misprint—the mileage is better in the city!).

Honda is rumored to be working on a hybrid mini-SUV, and other companies will likely follow with larger, more spacious hybrid vehicles.

Because hybrids are manufactured in fairly low quantities, you probably won't be able to stop by your local dealership and test-drive one, or buy it on a whim. Instead, you'll have to order one, pay full MSRP (see Chapter 3), and wait several weeks before it arrives. The upside of ordering your hybrid (or any vehicle, for that matter) is that you can name your color and options.

Luxury Cars

Like hybrids, the feature that connects the vehicles in this category isn't size or styling. Instead, luxury cars are grouped together because they're all expensive. With that expense, however, you get to drive a truly comfortable, high-performance vehicle: leather seats that glide into position when you step into the car, a smooth and quiet ride, soft leather on the steering wheel, plenty of interior room, and the following standard features: air conditioning with automatic climate control; power windows, door locks, and mirrors; keyless entry; advanced multi-speaker stereo system with CD player; and remote security system.

Not sure which cars fall into the "luxury" category? Chances are, you've heard of the following luxury car manufacturers:

- Acura
- Aston Martin
- Audi
- Bentley
- BMW
- Bugatti
- Cadillac
- Infinity
- Jaguar
- Lamborghini
- Land Rover
- Lexus
- Lincoln
- Mercedes-Benz
- Peugeot
- Rolls-Royce
- Saab
- Volvo

Go ahead and test drive models from any of these manufacturers to get a feel for what luxury is. You may decide not to buy or purchase any $45,000+ cars, but you'll have had the experience. If you do decide that you just have to have a luxury car, make sure you're buying or leasing it for a good reason, such as one of the following:

- You have more money than you know what to do with, and instead of buying another race horse or a house in Tuscany, you go shopping for a Bentley. More power to ya!
- You were already seriously considering leasing, and a luxury automobile will raise your down payment by only a few hundred dollars and your monthly payments by $50 or less. Go for it!
- Your plan is to purchase a vehicle every fifteen or twenty years, maintain it flawlessly, and drive it until its very last drop of oil. Because luxury cars tend to last longer than other cars, this is actually an incredibly wise—and frugal—decision.

If luxury vehicles are too pricey for you, consider an emerging vehicle category called near-luxury. These cars, priced from the high twenties to the low forties, have many of same qualities as luxury vehicles that rival the cost of a small house, so they're still very comfortable and attractive cars. If you think you may be interested in a near-luxury car, consider any of the following:

- Acura CL and TL
- Audi A4
- BMW 3-series
- Buick Park Avenue
- Cadillac Catera
- Chrysler 300M and LHS
- Infinity I30
- Jaguar X-Type
- Lexus ES300 and IS300
- Lincoln LS
- Mazda Millenia
- Mercedes-Benz C-Class
- Mitsubishi Diamante
- Oldsmobile Aurora
- Saab 9-3
- Toyota Avalon
- Volvo S60

Classic Cars

Classic cars are older cars that are in good shape, have low mileage, and are a joy to behold. They range from sporty Mustangs to old VW Beetles to luxurious Cadillacs. You don't buy a classic car for features or convenience—few have air conditioning, cruise control, or a port for your laptop—you buy them because you want to be transported to a different place and time.

Classic cars are more of a hobby than a purchase; in fact, many classic car owners keep (and work on) their cars in a garage and have different, newer vehicles that they use for everyday commuting and errands. If you're passionate about a particular type of older vehicle, can afford the extra insurance and garage space, and genuinely like to work on cars, a classic car may be an immensely enjoyable purchase. Keep yours buffed and shined, and bring it out for a spin with the top down on the sunniest days of the year.

For a well-designed Web site that's all about classic cars, visit *www.myclassiccar.com*. See Chapter 11 for listings of classic car museums and shows.

Concept Cars

Concept cars are vehicles that aren't ready to be mass produced and sold, but are shown at auto shows (see Chapter 10) as a peek at a potential product. Some become available for purchase; others do not.

The designs of these cars change frequently—in fact, concept cars don't have any one particular look. The unifying feature of concept cars is that they are rather funky and futuristic, so you get the "Wow!" factor when your car first hits the road. The most popular concept car today is the DaimlerChrysler PT Cruiser, although its novelty has already started to wear off and it's now being categorized as a station wagon or minivan. The Pontiac Aztec could also be considered a concept car because it's extremely unique, but with its four-wheel drive capability, it fits better into the SUV category.

chapter two

So Many Cars! Deciding Among Many

Even after you decide on a vehicle category (see Chapter 1), you still have far too many choices available to you. This chapter helps you continue to narrow your options by looking at how well the vehicles you're interested in perform in crash tests, establishing your price range, deciding whether to buy a new or used car, determining a vehicle's reliability and longevity (including how to steer clear of lemons), examining warranties, and looking at the factors that will either raise or lower your ongoing expenses: fuel efficiency and insurance.

Looking at Safety

Safety ratings of nearly all vehicles are available on the Internet, yet few people check those ratings before selecting a car, truck, minivan, or SUV to purchase or lease. Far too often, car buyers think only of costs and vehicle specifications, forgetting that traffic accidents are a leading cause of premature death in the United States.

I urge you to look closely at safety ratings, which are conducted by two separate nationwide organizations, before buying a vehicle. In addition to these ratings, find out whether the vehicles you're considering come with a driver's side airbag, a passenger airbag (which can be detached, should a young child need to ride in the passenger seat), side airbags, and side airbag head-protection systems. Ideally, you want all four of these types of airbags in your next vehicle.

National Highway Traffic Safety Administration Ratings

The National Highway Traffic Safety Administration (NHTSA) conducts the following three tests:

1. **Frontal crash rating:** Vehicles are rated by the chance of a thigh injury or life-threatening head or chest injury by occupants of the front seats. Occupants are assumed to use safety belts.
2. **Side crash rating:** Vehicles are rated by the chance of a pelvic injury or life-threatening chest injury by the driver and a rear-seat passenger on the driver's side. Occupants are assumed to use safety belts. This rating does not measure the chance of head injuries.
3. **Rollover resistance rating:** Vehicles are rated on their risk of rolling over in a single-vehicle crash, such as running off the road. This rating essentially measures how top-heavy a vehicle is, because top-heavy vehicles are more likely to roll over than other vehicles.

You can find the results of these tests, as well as other useful information, on NHTSA's Web site, at *www.nhtsa.dot.gov/cars/ testing.*

According to their recent findings, in frontal and side crash ratings only the 2001 Honda Civic two-door hatchback, the Volvo S-80 four-door sedan, the Honda Odyssey minivan, and the Ford Windstar minivan received perfect scores. In addition, several other models of vehicles were nearly perfect in their front crash and side crash ratings.

The NHTSA notes that "vehicles are twice as likely to be involved in severe frontal crashes than in severe side crashes," so if you have to choose between the importance of the frontal crash rating or the side crash rating, choose the vehicle with the highest frontal crash rating. In addition, "rollovers have a higher fatality rate than other crashes," so be sure to pay close attention to that rating. Fortunately, more than half a dozen vehicles have received perfect rollover resistance scores.

Insurance Institute for Highway Safety

Another organization, the Insurance Institute for Highway Safety (IIHS), conducts a different set of tests, as follows:

1. **Frontal offset crash test:** This test evaluates the crash-worthiness of vehicles. The vehicle is subjected to a 40 mph front crash and is then measured as to how well it held up structurally.
2. **Low-speed (bumper) crash test:** In this test, a vehicle is subjected to four crashes at 5 mph to see how well the bumper protects the car body from minor damage.
3. **Head restraint test:** This tests measures how well the head restraint (also know as the head rest) stops an occupant's head from snapping back.

4. **Side impact test:** This test measures how well side airbags protect occupants' heads when the vehicle crashes into a pole or into the side of another vehicle.

For a complete listing of vehicles rated in these four categories, visit the IIHS at *www.hwysafety.org/vehicle_ratings/ratings.htm.* Choose a vehicle category and comparison-shop between models within that category. No vehicle has scored a "Good" rating on all four tests, although several cars received a "Good" on all but the bumper crash test—after all, bumper crashes may be expensive, but they are certainly not life-threatening.

Establishing a Price Range

This is a pretty simple idea: Decide how much you want to spend and don't go above that number. If you know how much you could afford each month but aren't sure how much vehicle that will get you, call your bank or credit union and a few car dealerships to find out what the going interest rate is for 36-, 48-, and 60-month loans. Then use the car payment calculator at *www.bankamerica.com* or *www.edmunds.com* and plug in several different total amounts to see what monthly payments pop up.

Whenever possible, finance your vehicle for no more than thirty-six months, so that you're never caught with an upside-down car loan (when you want to get rid of your car, but you owe more than it's worth). If you can't afford much of a vehicle, consider leasing (see Chapter 6), but keep in mind that at the end of the lease term, you won't own any part of your car and will have to lease or buy another. For either buying or leasing, you'll have to come up with a cash down payment or trade in another vehicle.

Buying New or Buying Used

A smart option if you're short on funds is to buy a used car. Follow the same decision-making procedures outlined in this chapter, but also determine how old a car you're willing to buy. Then search the Internet, classified ads, and used-car dealers' lots for the perfect vehicle.

The Advantages and Disadvantages of a New Car

The first major advantage of a new car is purely psychological. When buying a new car, you get to experience all the sights and sounds associated with a new, expensive toy. Think of the new-car smell, the gleaming paint job, and the excitement of pulling into your driveway with a new toy. You know that no one—not a single person—has mistreated the car before you owned it. And unlike buying a new computer or audio equipment, you don't have to spend hours fiddling with your new possession—you simply get in the car, start the ignition, and enjoy the ride.

The other major advantage to buying a new vehicle is much more practical: For no additional charge, you get a warranty that covers all major repairs for a limited amount of time. Some manufacturers offer this warranty for thirty-six months or 36,000 miles, whichever comes first, but a growing number of companies are offering warranties up to 100,000 miles. These warranties don't cover the cost of replacing items like your tires, brake pads, or oil, and don't include the cost of tune-ups. Warranties also don't include collision repairs that may stem from an accident, although your insurance should cover that expense. However, if any major system gives you problems during the life of your warranty, you simply take the car back to your dealer for repairs. See the "Examining Warranties" section, later in this chapter, for a listing of the warranties offered by the major vehicle manufacturers.

In addition, if your new car ends up having persistent defects, your vehicle may be covered by your state's lemon laws (see the "Understanding Lemon Laws" section of this chapter). New cars are also eligible for extended warranties, which you can purchase at an additional cost (see Chapter 3).

New leased cars, like new purchased cars, usually also carry manufacturer's warranties, so major repairs are covered by your dealer. Check your contract to be sure this is the case.

The primary disadvantage of new cars is their incredible expense. Most vehicle models lose about 50 percent of their value every four years. This isn't true of all vehicles, especially those that run well after ten or fifteen years and hundreds of thousands of miles, but is a useful rule to keep in mind. In fact, some people suggest that a new vehicle will lose twenty percent of its value the minute you drive it off the dealer's lot, and yet you're paying full price for it.

Advantages and Disadvantages of Buying a Used Car

Buying a used car is an alternative to paying an arm and a leg for a brand-new car. As leasing has grown in popularity, the supply of affordable, low-mileage cars has steadily grown. In addition, as manufacturers improve their process and make cars more reliable, cars are beginning to last years longer than they did a few decades ago. If you purchase a high-quality vehicle that's three, four, or five years old, you may still own it a decade, and you'll have paid much less for it than for a comparable new vehicle.

Monthly payments to purchase a used car are often lower than leasing payments for a similar model of a new car, and when your payments end, you own the car. Although it may not be worth a lot of money at that time, it will still be worth something—perhaps enough to make a substantial down payment on another vehicle.

Used cars do have two major disadvantages, however: One is that when you purchase a used car, especially one from an individual (as opposed to a dealer), your car may not be covered under any sort of warranty. If the car is new enough, you may be able to transfer the original manufacturer's warranty from the previous owner to you, but find out whether this is possible *before* agreeing to buy the car.

When you buy a used car from a dealer, you may be eligible for a warranty, though it will generally have a shorter life (generally, one year) than new-car warranties do. Also, a used-car warranty may be offered by the dealer instead of the vehicle manufacturer, which means that if you move from Tuscon to Boston, you may have trouble getting your repairs made. (See "Examining Warranties.") Used leased cars, which aren't very popular, often have no warranties.

The other disadvantage to buying a used car is that you have no history with the vehicle and cannot know for sure how well or poorly the previous owner(s) maintained it. To avoid problems, buy only vehicles that have written documentation (receipts from service stations) showing oil changes every 3,000 to 5,000 miles; tune-ups every 15,000 miles; and new tires, new brake pads on brakes, and new belts as needed. If you're buying from a dealer, you may not have access to this information, so don't shy away from buying a used car from an individual seller. If the seller tells you that he or she did all repairs without the help of a service station, though, beware! The seller may well know a lot about cars and did actually do the service, but without written receipts, you can't know for sure that the car has been well-maintained. And don't assume that it's a dream car because it has low mileage and was barely driven by someone's grandmother. Vehicles that have mostly sat in garages may not have had any maintenance work done at all, and you don't want your engine to seize up because your new-to-you car never had an oil change. Insist on maintenance records from your friend's grandmother, too.

To ensure that a car you're considering has been properly

maintained, make the sale of the car contingent on your mechanic's approval. You may need to pay a down payment to hold the car and have it delivered to your mechanic, but that's a reasonable expectation. Make sure you verbally agree with the seller that the deposit is refundable if your mechanic says the car doesn't pass muster and write "refundable deposit contingent on mechanic's approval" in the memo section of your check. Have the seller take the vehicle to your mechanic or ask the mechanic to pick up the vehicle.

One other way to be sure that a used vehicle has been properly maintained is to purchase a car you just leased. After you've leased a new car, the car becomes used—and, therefore, less expensive than it was when it was new—so carefully consider your option to buy your leased vehicle. How else can you be absolutely sure that the previous owner was good to the car?

Understanding Lemon Laws

Lemons are vehicles that continue to have the same problems over and over. This term generally applies to new cars that are under warranty, so you may wonder, "What's the big deal?" The first time your new car experiences a mechanical problem, you may simply take it back to the dealer for a repair and think nothing of it. The second time, however, you may start to worry that the problem goes deeper than the repair your dealer is making. By the third time, you've spent quite a bit of time at the service desk of your dealership and may have been stuck in some uncomfortable places as a result of mechanical failures. You're beginning to wonder why you bothered to buy a new car in the first place, when you could have spent half as much on a used car and had the same—or better—experience.

Several years ago, I purchased a new car and just a few weeks later, I found myself stranded in the parking lot after work, unable to start my car. The alternator was quickly going bad. I was able to get the car to the dealership pretty painlessly, and the service department replaced the alternator and sent me on my way. I didn't think about my alternator again until a few months later, when it died again. It happened when I was driving alone on an interstate late one night—all of a sudden, the car's headlights began to dim and the battery sign lit up. I had just enough time to pull up at a rest stop before my lights shut off and the car died. A friend drove three hours to pick me up, and through a lot of hassle, I was able to arrange for another dealership in that area to replace the alternator again.

By this time, I was upset and began researching my state's lemon laws. In my particular state, however, a problem had to occur four times and the car had to be out of commission for thirty days before the manufacturer would be forced to refund the car owner's money or provide another vehicle. Although the alternator died one last time—fortunately, when I was close to home—that was the last time, and I never qualified for a refund. For the remaining years that I owned that car, though, I never felt safe.

Although a federal law (the Magnuson-Moss Warranty Act) suggests that manufacturers should be given three attempts to repair problems or the car owner can take the manufacturer to court, most state laws allow for four attempts to repair the problem. In addition, most state laws require the car owner to show that the vehicle was out of service for at least thirty days as a result of the repairs, and most problems don't take more than a week for dealers to repair. As a result, lemon laws have not helped many consumers who have experienced repeated problems with their vehicles.

Your best bet for avoiding a lemon—whether you're buying a new or used car—is to do the following:

- Avoid purchasing a new model in its first year. If a man-ufacturer introduces a new car that you're taken with, give the manufacturer one year to work through the kinks before you buy that model.

- For just $24 per year or $3.95 per month, you have access to the *Consumer Reports* online product ratings, including detailed model-by-model evaluations of both new and used vehicles. Using this rating system, you get an opportunity to see which models are reliable and which you should avoid.
- Before buying any used car, refer to Autopedia's Car Fax Lemon Check at *http://wsf.carfax.com.* This free service allows you to type in the vehicle identification number (VIN) of any used car you're considering buying to see whether it has hidden problems.

Looking at Reliability and Longevity

Reliability refers to how often you'll have to repair your vehicle—the more reliable it is, the less likely it is to break down at an inconvenient time. Longevity, on the other hand, refers to how long a product will last, even with repeated use: Some cars will last for five or six years before they become more hassle to repair than they're worth; other cars can last for fifteen or twenty years before reaching that point. It is especially important to consider reliability and longevity when purchasing a used car.

Some vehicles cost more to maintain than others, because their parts are more expensive or repairs and maintenance take longer, costing more in labor. In general, foreign cars—especially luxury foreign cars—tend to cost the most to maintain. The MSN Carpoint Web site's Reliability Rating page rates the problems associated with various vehicle systems of a wide variety of vehicles. Visit *http://carpoint.msn.com/home/reliability_ratings.asp* to check on cars you are interested in purchasing or leasing.

Another great way to determine vehicle reliability is by checking the *Consumer Reports* Repair History charts for your make and model. A summary of the best and worst cars, rated by reliability, is available on its Web site *(www.consumerreports.org),* although you'll have to pay a subscription fee to see the details. This expense is well worth the detailed information you get.

Save Money on Repair Costs

Choosing a reliable, long-lasting vehicle will save you a lot of time and money on repair work down the road. In addition to making a smart purchase or leasing arrangement, you can save on repair costs by following these guidelines:

- Find a service station that you trust. If you aren't comfortable with the people working on your vehicle, go elsewhere. Ask friends, coworkers, and family where they take their vehicles. You never want to feel as though you're being taken for a ride.
- Read your owner's manual to find out how often your manufacturer recommends getting oil changes—and then follow this advice. A general rule is one oil change every 5,000 miles if you drive mostly highway miles; once very 3,000 miles if you make mostly short trips or drive on dusty roads. To really save wear and tear on your engine and also improve your car's resale value, get the oil changed every 3,000 miles—it'll usually cost you less than $25 but will make your car last longer.
- Whenever you get an oil change, ask to have the air filter replaced, too.
- Every two oil changes, ask to have the fuel filter (sometimes called the gas filter) replaced.
- When replacing major parts, make sure they're made by your manufacturer—so if you're driving a Ford, use genuine

Ford parts. This probably means you'll have to have your vehicle serviced at a dealer instead of an independent service station, but as a result, you'll be using parts that are made to fit the exact specifications of your vehicle.

- Up to 20,000 miles, get your vehicle serviced every 5,000 miles. After your 30,000-mile major tune-up, get a minor tune-up and inspection every 15,000 miles and a major tune-up and inspection every 30,000. You'll spend a few hundred dollars on these tune-ups but will save yourself a bundle in major repairs by preventing major damage to critical parts.
- Use the grade of gasoline recommended by your owner's manual.

Remember to keep good records—including receipts—for all vehicle maintenance. Proven records of every single bit of maintenance you've done will make your car more valuable when you sell it.

If you want to save a boatload of money, purchase vehicles that tend to last through many years and hundreds of thousands of miles—and then actually keep them as long as you can stand to. A Volvo, for example, has an average life expectancy of over eighteen years! While your upfront cost for a Volvo is pretty high—an average of roughly $30,000—if you keep it for eighteen years, you're paying less than $1,700 per year for a vehicle. If, on the other hand, you buy a $20,000 car that will be on its last legs after six years (and many cars fall into this category), you're paying over $3,000 per year for your car.

One way to determine which vehicles last the longest is to look at ratings and prices of used cars: The higher the average price of a used car, the more likely it is to last for years and years. Check out the Kelley Blue Book for a guide to used car prices, or visit *www.kbb.com*.

Longevity is irrelevant if you're leasing a vehicle, unless you plan to purchase the vehicle after your lease term is over. If you lease vehicles for just two or three years and then trade them in for another, how long the vehicle may last won't really matter to you.

Examining Warranties

Every vehicle comes with a warranty, but they differ in length and breadth of coverage. Standard warranties, which last for three years or 36,000 miles—whichever comes first—cover just about every part of the vehicle, although stereo and CD players and tires may have separate warranties or no coverage at all. Powertrain warranties, which generally last longer than basic warranties, protect the engine, transmission, and related mechanisms. Many companies also offer a corrosion warranty, which covers damage from rust. Table 2-1 compares the standard, powertrain, and corrosion warranties of the major automobile manufacturers.

Table 2-1
Warranty Information (Years/Miles)

Make	Standard	Powertrain	Corrosion
Acura	4/50,000	4/50,000	5/unlimited
Audi	4/50,000	4/50,000	12/unlimited
BMW	4/50,000	4/50,000	6/unlimited
Buick	3/36,000	3/36,000	6/100,000
Cadillac	4/50,000	4/50,000	6/100,000
Chevrolet	3/36,000	3/36,000	5/100,000

Table 2-1 *(continued)*
Warranty Information (Years/Miles)

Make	Standard	Powertrain	Corrosion
Daewoo	3/36,000	5/60,000	5/unlimited
DaimlerChrysler	3/36,000	3/36,000	6/100,000
Dodge	3/36,000	3/36,000	5/100,000
Ford	3/36,000	3/36,000	5/unlimited
GMC	3/36,000	3/36,000	6/100,000
Honda	3/36,000	3/36,000	5/unlimited
Hyundai	5/60,000	10/100,000	5/100,000
Infiniti	4/60,000	6/70,000	7/unlimited
Isuzu	3/50,000	10/120,000	6/100,000
Jaguar	4/50,000	4/50,000	6/unlimited
Jeep	3/36,000	3/36,000	5/100,000
Kia	5/60,000	10/100,000	5/100,000
Land Rover	4/50,000	4/50,000	6/unlimited
Lexus	4/50,000	6/70,000	6/unlimited
Lincoln	4/50,000	4/50,000	5/unlimited
Mazda	3/50,000	3/50,000	5/unlimited
Mercedes-Benz	4/50,000	4/50,000	4/50,000
Mercury	3/36,000	3/36,000	5/unlimited
Mitsubishi	3/36,000	5/60,000	7/100,000
Nissan	3/36,000	5/60,000	5/unlimited
Oldsmobile	5/60,000	5/60,000	6/100,000
Pontiac	3/36,000	3/36,000	6/100,000
Porsche	4/50,000	4/50,000	10/unlimited
Saab	4/50,000	4/50,000	6/unlimited
Saturn	3/36,000	3/36,000	6/100,000
Subaru	3/36,000	5/60,000	5/unlimited
Suzuki	3/36,000	3/36,000	3/unlimited
Toyota	3/36,000	5/60,000	5/unlimited
Volkswagen	4/50,000	5/60,000	12/unlimited
Volvo	4/50,000	4/50,000	8/unlimited

As you narrow your list of potential vehicles, compare warranties, even on used cars. Used-car warranties are often backed by the dealer, not the manufacturer, so if you're thinking of moving out of the area in the next couple of years, ask whether you can transfer your used-car warranty to another dealer. Most used-car warranties are quite short, from six to twenty-four months.

If you're buying a new vehicle but plan to sell it a few years from now, ask your dealer whether the warranties can be transferred to a new owner.

Warranties don't cover the cost of replacing your tires (which usually have their own short warranty, usually just twelve months), brake pads, and oil, and don't include the cost of tune-ups. Warranties also don't include collision repairs that may stem from an accident. Some manufacturers, however, offer free roadside assistance for anywhere from two to five years.

Analyzing Fuel Efficiency

To really save money, choose a car with the highest fuel efficiency you can find. With fluctuating gas prices constantly threatening to rise even higher, you can save a bundle by choosing a high-mileage vehicle. If, for example, you drive 200 miles per week and gas is $1.70 per gallon, you'll spend $884 per year on gasoline with a car that gets twenty miles to the gallon. Choose a car that gets thirty-five miles to the gallon, and you'll spend just $505 per year on gasoline. Over five years, you'll save $1,894 on gasoline costs alone!

One tip to keep in mind: Although they're a pain to learn to drive, cars with manual transmissions (stick shifts) get better gas mileage than cars with automatic transmissions.

Scrutinizing Insurance Costs

Believe it or not, your annual insurance costs can vary by hundreds—sometimes even thousands—of dollars based on which type of vehicle you purchase. As you narrow your choices to three to five models, call or e-mail your insurance agent to find out how much each will cost to insure and determine how much you'll save over the life of your vehicle by choosing the cheapest. Some insurance companies may have this information available to their customers online or by phone. For instance, if you register at Progressive Casualty Insurance Company's Web site (at *www.personalprogressive.com*), you'll be able to get instant insurance quotes for cars you are considering to purchase or lease.

Other ways you can save on insurance include the following:

- **Avoid tickets and accidents.** Each time you receive a ticket or are responsible for an auto accident, you insurance premiums will go up. And even if you're not at fault in accidents but you have been in several, your premiums may increase because of your tendency to be accident-prone.
- **Drive a safe vehicle.** The higher a vehicle ranks in safety tests, the less chance you and your passengers have of sustaining serious injury, which, in turn, means you're less of a risk to an insurance company.
- **Get credit for auto safety features, such as antilock brakes, air bags, and so on.** Be sure to tell your agent about these features—don't assume he or she will know that your car has them.
- **Drive an inexpensive car.** The less your car costs to replace, the less your insurance company will charge you to insure it.
- **Live close to your workplace.** Insurance companies figure you'll have fewer opportunities to get into accidents.
- **Join an auto club (like AAA).** Besides offering roadside assistance and towing, maps and tour books, free traveler's cheques, and other useful products, some auto clubs also offer reasonable insurance rates.

- **Raise your deductible.** With many companies, deductibles are automatically set at $250 unless you change them. This means that if your car is stolen, vandalized, or damaged in an accident, you'll pay the first $250 of repairs, and your insurance company will pay the rest. If you're willing (and able) to pay more than that, raise your deductible to $500 or $1,000. Your insurance premiums will go way down.

  If having a higher premium makes you nervous, consider starting a savings account with an amount equal to your deductible. If you need to pay the deductible, you're assured that you have the money. If you put all your insurance deductibles (medical, homeowner's, and so on) into one account and you're fortunate enough to not have any claims for a few years, you may start earning enough interest to help pay your premiums.

- **Drop your collision insurance.** If you're paying a lot for insurance and you drive an older car that is worth less than $1,000 or $1,500 dollars, you may be able to save several hundred dollars per year by dropping your collision insurance altogether. Remember, though, that this means your insurance company will *not* reimburse you for the damages incurred to your vehicle if you get into an accident. Also be sure that your state laws permit driving without collision insurance.

- **Ask whether your occupation gets you a discount.** Workers in some professions receive discounts on auto insurance from the insurance company. The list of professions varies from company to company, so ask your agent whether your particular profession makes you eligible for a discount. If you're a student, keep in mind that some insurance companies offer discounts for getting good grades.

- **Own a home.** Apparently, this demonstrates stability and responsibility to insurance companies, but really has nothing to do with your driving skills.
- **Combine your auto insurance with your homeowner's insurance.** By insuring both major purchases with one company, you may earn a multiple-policy discount.

Choosing Between American-Made and Foreign Cars

Choosing between an American-made and foreign car is a tricky business, and one that is largely a personal decision.

I grew up outside of Detroit—the Motor City—where driving a foreign car is about as acceptable as passing gas in an elevator. When I was younger, I heard anecdotes from GM and Ford employees who had to park in the farthest spots from the buildings in which they worked (sometimes as much as a mile away) because they drove foreign cars. And in times of economic hardship, driving an American-made vehicle—much like wearing American-made clothing—has always been a source of national pride.

But now, many American automobile manufacturers either own or have joint ventures with foreign car manufacturers. Look at the following examples:

- General Motors (GM) owns Chevrolet, Pontiac, Buick, Oldsmobile, Cadillac, GMC, Saturn, Hummer, Saab, Opel, Vauxhall, and Holden; and has joint ventures with Toyota, Renault, Subaru, and Suzuki.
- Ford owns Lincoln, Mercury, Mazda, Volvo, Jaguar, Aston Martin, and Land Rover; and has a joint venture with Nissan.
- DaimlerChrysler owns Dodge, Jeep, and Mercedes-Benz; and has an alliance with Mitsubishi and Hyundai.

Judging from the preceding list, you may have trouble sorting the "American" automakers from the "foreign" ones. On the flipside, BMW, Honda, Isuzu, Mazda, Mercedes-Benz, Nissan, and Toyota own manufacturing plants in the United States and employ tens of thousands of American workers to produce their vehicles.

Creating a Vehicle-Selection Matrix

After you've chosen a particular category and have researched several vehicles in that category, you're ready to test-drive a handful of new or used vehicles and determine which will appear on your final list of three or so vehicles.

After driving each car and taking home all the full-color brochures the salesperson will offer, complete the following Vehicle-Selection Matrix to make your final decision. Here's how the matrix, shown in Table 2-2, works:

1. For each vehicle feature listed (and you can add a couple more, if you wish), determine how important that feature is to you by rating the feature from one (not important) to five (critical).
2. Write the name of each make and model you're considering under "Vehicle #1," "Vehicle #2," and so on.
3. Rate the first vehicle based on each feature, from one (not so great) to five (passes with flying colors), and place that number in the left-hand column.
4. Multiply the importance rating by the vehicle rating to get a total in the right-hand column.
5. Repeat for the other vehicles.
6. Total each of the three right-hand columns. The column with the highest number is your final selection.

Table 2-2
Vehicle-Selection Matrix

Vehicle Features	Importance to You		
	Vehicle #1	Vehicle #2	Vehicle #3
Comfort			
Safety			
Price			
Maintenance costs			
Reliability			
Warranty			
Fuel efficiency			
Insurance costs			
American/foreign			
Passenger space			
Cargo space			
Appearance			
TOTALS			

chapter three

How Much Do Cars Really Cost and How Little Can You Pay?

Although every vehicle is given a suggested price by manufacturers, the price you pay for a given model can vary by thousands of dollars, depending on how well you do your homework and how assertive you choose to be. This chapter tells you how to find out how much the dealer is paying for any new vehicle on the market, which will arm you with enough information to be able to get a fantastic deal on your next car. To find out how to negotiate with a salesperson after you know how much you should spend, take a look at Chapter 5.

Note that while this chapter is geared toward buyers of new cars, many of the tips and tricks are useful for new-car leasers (who must negotiate a price for their leased cars) and used-car buyers.

Recognizing the MSRP
and Dealer Sticker Price

MSRP stands for manufacturer's suggested retail price—the price that dealers and manufacturers hope you'll pay for their cars. In addition to the MSRP, manufacturers charge a destination fee for shipping the vehicle from the manufacturer to the dealer. (This standard charge is available on manufacturers' Web sites and shouldn't be altered by the dealer.)

Together, the MSRP and destination charge make up the sticker price, named for the Monroney sticker you'll find on the window of every new vehicle. If you were to walk into a dealership and plunked down the sticker price, you could drive the car off the lot within a few minutes. But you don't want to do that.

In order to pay much less than the sticker price, you first have to examine the Monroney sticker, which tells you exactly what equipment comes standard on the vehicle; that is, the equipment included in the base price (the cost of the car with standard equipment and without additional options).

The Monroney sticker also lists the optional equipment—along with prices—that has been installed on the car. This optional, factory-installed equipment, such as air conditioning, cruise control, manual transmission, and anti-lock brakes, is often bundled in a trim package that includes several features at a reduced price. Generally, you can't remove these features from the car because they're installed at the factory. You do have the option of ordering a car that doesn't include the extra features. However, by ordering a car directly from the manufacturer and not buying one that's on a dealer's lot, you may lose bargaining power. Dealers are more likely to negotiate when a car has been sitting on the lot for several months.

The Monroney sticker may list one other type of equipment: dealer options that were not installed at the factory but were added at the dealership. These types of options include rust-proofing and sealant, racing stripes, and other features that don't add to the value of your car, but may cost several hundred dollars.

By totaling the base price, destination charge, factory-installed options, and dealer-installed options, the Monroney sticker lists what's known as the dealer sticker price, which is roughly the equivalent of a price tag on an antique dresser at a flea market: It's just a starting point.

Understanding What the Dealer Pays

One of the most important pieces of information you can arm yourself with is the dealer cost: the price that the dealer pays the manufacturer for a particular vehicle with its factory-installed options. This cost, also called the invoice price, is one that the dealer knows you have access to and will use to gain your sympathies. The dealer may say something like, "The price you're suggesting is just fifty dollars over invoice—don't you think we deserve to make more than fifty bucks on each car?" Hard to argue with that, isn't it? After all, the dealer invoice is often a few thousand dollars less than the sticker price, so you may think that the price the dealer is offering ($50 over invoice) is as low as the he or she can go.

What dealers don't want you to know about are dealer incentives or holdbacks, which usually amount to between 2 and 3 percent of the MSRP and are provided by the manufacturers to dealers. These incentives may allow the dealer to pay the manufacturer less than the invoice price, which means that if you pay less than invoice, the dealer could still make a profit. What this amounts to is that you should never, never, never, never pay MSRP, no matter how much you loathe negotiating, and you may be able to pay the dealer invoice amount—or less!

Where to Find the MSRP and Dealer Costs

To find the MSRP (retail) and dealer cost (invoice), log onto the Kelley Blue Book Web site at *www.kbb.com.* Click on New Car Pricing, enter your zip code, and click Continue. From there, select a vehicle category, select a make, and click on the model and configuration you're interested in. You can also visit Edmunds.com at *www.edmunds.com* for similar information.

When I logged onto the Kelley Blue Book site and asked to see prices for a Honda CR-V LX with four-wheel drive and a five-speed transmission, I received the following information: The retail price (MSRP), including the destination fee, is $19,590, and the invoice is $17,942. I'm told that Honda is offering 3.9 percent financing for the next six weeks, and look at a list of standard equipment, including air conditioning, power door locks, cruise control, rear window defroster and wiper/washer, rear mud guards, and so on. The standard equipment includes everything I want, so the next step is deciding on a price I'm comfortable with.

The 2001 dealer holdback list at *www.edmunds.com* tells me that Honda offers my dealer 2 percent of the MSRP, so they'll receive nearly $400 even if they sell the car to me at the invoice price. That seems like a reasonable amount of money for each car they sell, so I decide that a reasonable cost for a new Honda CRV is roughly $18,000—but that's the most I want to pay. If I can get the dealer to accept earning $100 on the deal instead of $400, even better. So, I decide to visit the new-car Web sites (listed in Chapter 5) and see how many come in at $17,700 or less. But I also know that I'm willing to pay as much as $18,000. (Chapter 5 will also show you how to get a dealer to agree to this price.)

But here's what actually happened: One dealer came back with a price of $17,500—which should be a loss ($17,942 invoice minus $400 holdback is $17,542). Hmmm. Because this exchange came at the end of the model year, perhaps Honda was offering a better holdback this month than is shown on the dealer holdback list. The point is that you don't want to set your price too high: Aim to pay dealer invoice (at the highest) and dealer invoice minus the holdback (at the lowest). But be sure to let the dealer make *some* money to pay commissions, building and utility expenses, taxes, and so on.

Knowing the dealer holdback is critical for negotiating the lowest possible price. A newsletter called *CarDeals* lists dealer incentives and holdbacks approximately twice per month, but getting a copy of that newsletter isn't easy. The company is supposed to have a Web site at *www.cardeals.com,* but it's often out of service. For $26, you can get a recent copy of *CarDeals,* plus a bunch of other articles and relevant information, from FightingChance.com at *www.fightingchance.com.* Likewise, *Automotive News* offers a list of dealer incentives and holdbacks each month. Although you can't get this information online, you can visit the magazine's Web site at *www.automotivenews.com* for information on how to subscribe to the magazine.

Looking for Cash Back and Financing Specials

Cash back and rebates refer to incentives from manufacturers that are returned to you after you purchase a vehicle, while special finance rates refer to low interest rates that the financing arm of major vehicle manufacturers is prepared to offer for certain vehicles. Sometimes, these customer incentives are either/or; that is, you either get the cash back or the special financing. When you have to choose between the two, calculate how much you'll pay in finance charges at the special rate and compare that amount to how much you'll pay if you finance your car through your local credit union or bank. If the savings don't equal the value of the cash back, choose the cash. Be sure to ask your dealer to apply the cash back to the price of the car—you'll save a little money when you go to pay your sales tax on the vehicle.

Manufacturers frequently advertise cash back offers, as well as other incentives. To find out what customer incentives may be available to you, pay attention to television commercials, check your local paper, or visit the Web site of the manufacturer of the vehicle you're interested in.

Avoiding Dealer-Supplied Financing

If you find a manufacturer's finance rate that's exceedingly low (anything under 6 percent), and you're planning to finance your vehicle, contact the financing arm of the manufacturer directly to find out how you can prequalify for the car you plan to buy. Taking this step removes the dealer from the details of your vehicle financing.

If your manufacturer isn't offering an impressive finance rate, know what finance rate your credit union, local banks, and online loan centers (see Chapter 8) are offering before you go to the dealership. If the dealer's rate is higher than what you can get elsewhere, don't finance at the dealership just to save the hassle of going elsewhere. Dealers can give you everything you ask for on the price of your new car, and then turn around and make thousands of dollars by charging you two extra percentage points on your loan.

Steering Clear of Dealer Prep Charges

If a dealer tells you—over the phone, via e-mail, or on the Monroney sticker that you have to pay a dealer prep fee, say, "No, thank you." A dealer prep charge is a fee for preparing a car for sale. Sounds legit, right? Well, it's not. The dealers are paid by the manufacturer to prepare the car for sale, so when unsuspecting customers pay this fee, the amount is simply added profit for dealers.

Passing Up Dealer-Installed Options

If you can avoid it, don't pay for dealer-installed options, which include everything from rust-proofing and cell phones to security systems and CD players. Dealers have a tremendous markup on these items, and you'll save plenty of money by avoiding these options (most vehicles are warranted against corrosion, so do you really need additional rustproofing?) or getting them installed after the sale at a specialty shop (a good idea for a security system and an audio system). For gimmicky add-ons that the dealer claims can't be removed, refuse to pay for them or move along to another dealership.

Sidestepping Portions of a Trim Package That You Don't Need

If you want everything offered in a trim package—for example, antilock brakes, cruise control, air conditioning, and pinstriping— you'll pay less for all four options in the trim package than you would if you bought each option separately. But don't pay a few thousand dollars for a trim package that gives you only one or two options you really want. See whether your dealer has other configurations of your car available, and if not, check with other dealers.

The manufacturer's Web site of the vehicle you have in mind likely lists the MSRP of each available option and of trim packages, so add up what you're getting and see whether the price is worthwhile. If not, move along to another dealership.

Staying Away from Extended Warranties/Service Contracts

Extended warranties, also known as service contracts, give you a longer warranty—more years and more miles—than the one provided by the vehicle manufacturer. To avoid paying your dealer any more than you have to, begin by looking carefully at the warranty that comes with your car (see Chapter 2 for a list of standard warranty provisions). Manufacturers have been falling all over themselves to offer the longest and broadest warranties, so you may find that you're looking at a car that comes standard with an eight-year, 100,000-mile warranty. And that may be plenty.

If the car you're thinking of purchasing has only a three-year, 36,000-mile warranty, you may want to purchase an extended warranty, but not from your dealer! Dealers have been known to sell $500 extended warranty packages for $1,500. For a much more reasonable extended warranty package, contact Warranty Direct at *www.warrantydirect.com/index.asp* or Warranty Gold at *www.warrantygold.com/carinfo/*. Keep in mind that for most new cars, an extended warranty must be purchased within a year of buying your vehicle.

Selling Your Old Vehicle Instead of Trading It In

Although trading in your old vehicle and applying the profits to your new vehicle seems easy, you'll likely receive far less money from a dealer than you would selling your existing car on your own. If you've been particularly persistent in your negotiations for a new car, any dealer worth his or her salt will try to earn back some of those lost profits by offering you far less for your old car than it's worth. And because you'll be nearing the end of your negotiations (and feeling pretty proud of yourself for getting the price you wanted on your new car), you may agree to the lower trade-in price out of sheer fatigue. Don't do it! You wouldn't pay $1,500 more than you have to for a new car, so don't take $1,500 less than you should for your old one.

Instead, before you're ready to buy your new vehicle, advertise your old one in your local paper, regional automotive classified paper, or online. Advertise for the private party value listed in the Kelley Blue Book *(www.kbb.com)* and see whether you get any bites. If not, lower the price a few hundred dollars and re-advertise.

If you sell your car, you can immediately head to your dealership with cash in hand. If you advertise for several weeks, however, and you don't get the price you want, you at least have a figure in mind when you head to the dealership with your trade-in.

Pricing Used Cars

Since the advent of the Internet, pricing used cars has never been easier. Most Web sites allow you to enter not only the year, make, and model, but a host of information about standard and optional equipment, and the condition of any vehicle you're searching for. The following sites are excellent sources—check several of them, and if the suggested prices are substantially different, use an average of all of them.

- Kelley Blue Book used-car prices: *www.kbb.com*
- Auto Trader used-car information: *www.autoconnect.com*
- Edmund's buying guides and pricing: *www.edmunds.com*
- IntelliChoice pricing information: *www.intellichoice.com*
- N.A.D.A. appraisal guides: *www.nadaguides.com*
- Pace price guides: *www.carprice.com*

chapter four

Knowing When to Buy and When to Lease

When you glance through the automotive advertisements in your Sunday paper, you may see vehicle prices that are sky high—often $30,000 to $35,000—and monthly payments that are surprisingly low—sometimes as little as $199 per month. How can that be?

Although you can take up to six years to make monthly payments on your vehicle, you still can't buy a $30,000 car for $199 per month, no matter how low your finance rate is and how much cash back the manufacturer offers. If you find a low monthly payment on an expensive vehicle, you're probably looking at a vehicle lease, which is an alternative to buying.

When you buy a vehicle, you pay cash or finance the cost of the car at a specific interest rate for a certain number of years. After you've paid the purchase price, you own the vehicle and can do with it what you want—sell it, paint it with racing stripes, put tens of thousands of miles on it as you drive across the country, or leave fast-food packages and other junk on the floor. The car belongs to you.

When you lease a car, however, you're borrowing it for a specified number of months or years. At the end of your contract, you have to give it back. Think of leasing like a long-term car rental: You can't sell the car or paint your name onto the hood, you have to watch your mileage, and you have to carry darned good insurance on the car so that you can pay the people who do own it, should you get into an accident. You can hang fuzzy dice from rearview mirror, but if you let your puppy ride in the car and he tears up the upholstery, you know it's gonna cost you. At the same time, however, leasing does have some advantages. This chapter helps you decide whether you want to lease or buy your next vehicle.

The Differences in Upfront, Monthly, and Long-Term Costs

In the short term, leasing a vehicle is much less expensive than buying one, because you are paying only enough to use the car, not to buy it. In the long term, however, you make payments for a number of month or years and have nothing to show for it at the end—the car belongs to the company who leased it to you. If you plan to always lease a vehicle (for the rest of your life), you'll always have to make a monthly lease payment—but you'll also be able to drive a new vehicle every few years.

When you buy a car, you make payments for a certain number of months or years, and then you own the vehicle. At that point, you can keep driving it and not make any car payments at all, or you can buy a new car and use your existing one as a substantial down payment on the new one. Many people keep driving their paid-off cars and keep paying their monthly payments to their own savings accounts. They then use this money, along with the money from the sale of their existing vehicles, as a substantial down payment for a new car. Eventually, they get to the point where they can pay cash for vehicles, saving thousands of dollars in finance charges.

Ultimately, you have to decide for yourself which arrangement will work best for your wallet. The following sections should help you make up your mind.

Down Payment

When you buy a car, your down payment is usually higher than it is when leasing a vehicle. Unless you're buying your first car, you can probably use your existing car as a down payment (also called a trade-in) and not have to come up with any cash at all. If you have recently financed your existing car, however (say you got a five-year loan, and you're eighteen months into it), the amount you owe on your loan (your payoff) may be higher than the value of the car. This situation is known as being upside-down on your loan. And if you don't own a vehicle that you're willing to sell or trade in, you usually have to come up with 5 to 20 percent of the price of the car as a down payment.

For a lease, you can also trade in an existing car or pay the down payment in cash. This is not a down payment against the cost of the vehicle, though, but against the cost of the lease. Just because you made a down payment doesn't mean that you'll own a part of the vehicle at the end of the lease term. This down payment varies greatly, but can run as little as zero dollars and as much as $3,000. When you lease a vehicle, you also have to provide a security deposit, just as you have to do when you rent an apartment. Often, this amount is equal to the first and last month's payments and is refundable at the end of the lease term.

Monthly Payments

When you buy a vehicle, your monthly payments add up to the price of the vehicle, plus interest. If, for example, you buy a $22,000 car, make an $8,000 trade-in, and are able to get a 7-percent interest rate, you'll pay $432 per month for thirty-six months (three years). At the end of three years, you'll own the car and can keep driving it without making any payments for as long as the car lasts. If you buy that same car with the same down payment and interest rate but spread the payments out for sixty months (five years), you'll pay just $277 per month. At the end of five years, you'll own the car free and clear, but it'll be worth less than it was two years (and many thousands of miles) earlier.

When you lease a car, you don't actually pay for the price of the car. Instead, you pay for the opportunity to drive it for two, three, or four years. The company leasing you the car (the lessor), needs to charge you enough so that it can sell the car at the end of your lease term and make just as much money, by combining your lease payments with the selling price of the now-used car, as it would have if it had sold the car new. Because you're not paying for the car itself, your monthly payments may be substantially lower. To lease a $22,000 car with $2,000 down (plus a $500 security deposit), you'll pay about $275 per month for twenty-four months, just a little less than what you'd pay for a five-year loan to buy the car. Of course, at the end of two years, you won't own the car, but if your lease contract gives you an option to buy, you can purchase the vehicle by going through traditional financing and making payments for several more months or years.

What leasing means for many people is that they can afford more car for the same monthly payment. A vehicle that costs $30,000 may have the same lease payments as the payments to buy a $20,000 car. Be sure, however, to see the long view: After you begin leasing cars, you may have difficultly ever going back to owning them. You won't be able to use a current car to make a down payment on your next car, so you'll always be shelling out new down payments for new cars—and never getting back that money and the amount you pay in monthly payments. And if you do decide to buy a car with monthly payments, you may find that the car you can afford doesn't have the GPS system and eight-speaker CD player, which you've gotten so used to.

You can reduce your monthly lease payments by paying a higher lease down payment. Before you sign a lease contract, ask how much of a difference an extra $100 or $1,000 toward your down payment will make in your monthly lease payments.

Resale Value

Although you don't usually pay quite as much to lease a car as you would to buy it, you don't own the car at the end of the lease term. Of course, that also means you don't have to mess with selling your vehicle on your own or negotiating a trade-in value at a car dealership (see "Trading In a Vehicle" in Chapter 8). As soon as you've made all your payments, you can hand your keys to your lessor and start shopping for a new car to lease. You'll get your security deposit back (and can use it toward the security deposit for your new car) and will have to make another down payment, but you're also driving a new car!

If you buy your car instead of leasing it, you own the car at the end of the lease term and can sell it or trade it in as down payment for a new car. Cars depreciate with time, however, which means that the older a car is and the more mileage it has on it, the less it's worth. The longer your financing term, then, the less your car will be worth when you go to sell it or trade it in at the end of the term.

Obtaining Credit

If you have a poor credit history, you may have an easier time obtaining a lease than a loan. A lessor is qualifying you only to use a vehicle, not buy it, and because your monthly payments are usually lower than when buying a car, you may qualify for a lease—and improve your credit history during the leasing period.

If you're set on buying a vehicle and don't have a spotless credit history, opt for an inexpensive car and save enough money to make a large down payment. If you're able to put down 20 or 30 percent of the price of the vehicle, you'll likely get the loan you want. And as a bonus, your monthly payments will be much lower than for an expensive car with a small down payment.

Ending Your Lease or Payment Contract Early

When you buy a car, you can get out of your contract in two ways: by trading your car in for another or by selling your vehicle and using the cash to pay off your loan balance. The finance company uses your vehicle as collateral, which is a guarantee of repayment—if you don't make your payments, they take away your vehicle. So, technically, if you sell your car to someone else and still owe money to your finance company, you have breached your contract, even if you plan to mail a check to the finance company later that day. Before you sell a car that you still owe payments on, contact your finance company for instructions on how to proceed.

When you trade in your car for another, however, the dealership takes care of paying off the loan for you. Be careful, however, that you're not upside-down in your loan—if you owe more than your car's worth, and you're absolutely sure that you want to purchase a new vehicle, you may have to pay the difference, in cash, between the payoff amount and the value of the car. Sometimes, the dealership will include that payoff difference in your new loan, but that means you're paying off an old, traded-in car at the same time that you're paying off a new car.

On the other hand, to end a lease before the lease term ends, you'll probably have to pay a large early termination fee, or you may be told that you simply can't terminate the lease. Some people try to sublease their vehicles, which means that another individual takes over payments on the lease through the end of the lease term. While this may be a useful solution, your contract may not allow subleasing. Before you sign a lease contract, make sure you know the consequences of changing your mind!

The Differences in Maintenance Costs

Many people are under the impression that because leased cars are owned by the lessor and not the lessee (that's you), they don't have to be maintained or repaired. Not true. With nearly all vehicle leases (and there are a few exceptions), you still have to pay for regular maintenance, including oil changes and tune-ups. Not everyone does, and this affects the condition of the car at the end of the lease term, but you're supposed to!

Many leased vehicles aren't covered by state lemon laws (see Chapter 2), so if you end up with a car that has persistent defects, you may have to live with them until the end of your lease.

The Differences in How Many Miles You Can Drive

When you buy a car, you can put as many miles on it as your heart desires, so if you choose to commute 100 miles every day or you take a vacation across the country once or twice a year, no one's going to stop you. The price you pay, however, is that higher-mileage vehicles aren't worth as much as their low-mileage counterparts, so down the road, your car won't be worth as much as it would if you never drove it outside your city limits.

For this same reason, leased cars come with an allowance of miles—usually 12,000 to 15,000 per year—and if you drive more than that, you pay a per-mile charge at the end of the lease term. That charge can be as much as twenty-five cents per mile over your allowable mileage! The rationale for this is that, at the end of your lease term, the lessor will have a used car to sell, and a used car with lots of miles is worth less than a used car with few miles. The lessor, then, makes you pay for the reduced value of the vehicle.

In addition to making you pay for excess miles, you may also have to pay a fee if your vehicle has excess wear and tear or damage. Check your contract for details and make sure you understand how your lessor defines "excess wear and tear" and "damage." You don't want to find out in three years that letting your muddy dog ride in the backseat of your leased SUV is going to cost you $500.

Buy Versus Lease Calculators

On the Internet, you can find a number of useful calculators that help you determine whether buying or leasing is a better financial decision for you. Check out the following sites:

- Mortgage-Calc.com: *www.mortgage-calc.com*
- Autoweb.com: *www.autoweb.com/calculator/* (click on "Loan vs. Lease")
- Kiplinger.com: *www.calcbuilder.com*

Keep in mind, however, that these calculators don't take into account certain personal financial decisions, like wanting to be debt-free, planning to retire early, going from two incomes to one in order for one parent to stay home with children, saving money for college or for a down payment on a house, and so on. If your goal is to drive a hip new car every couple of years without a lot of hassle, leasing may be your best bet. But if you want to spend less and save more—especially in the long term—buy a high-quality, reliable car on the fewest number of monthly payments you can afford, drive the car for eight to ten years, and sock money away during the years you aren't making car payments.

chapter five

Negotiating for Your Next Vehicle

Negotiating, which simply means "making business arrangements," doesn't have to be difficult or frightening. And it doesn't have to change your basic personality, even if your general nature is to be shy and nonconfrontational. Armed with the information you gathered in Chapter 3, true negotiation is about stating your needs, listening carefully to your dealer's needs, and then coming to an agreement or deciding not to agree. True negotiation has nothing to do with hurting people's feelings, being belligerent, yelling, or getting your way all the time.

This chapter shows you how to negotiate the old-fashioned way—in person at a local dealership—or the e-commerce way—by finding and bargaining with dealers over the Internet.

Doing Your Homework

Never go into a negotiation without information. If you haven't already read Chapter 3, I suggest you read it now before going any further in this chapter. Use the suggestions in that chapter to find out as much information as you can about the vehicle you have in mind, the cost of the vehicle to you and the dealer, the incentives that may be available to you and the dealer, and so on.

Steering Clear of "No-Haggle" Dealers

If reading a little of this chapter on negotiating is already making you tired, you may think the sound of a "no-haggle" dealership couldn't be sweeter. There, you may imagine, you can chat with nice people who don't pressure you to buy, look leisurely at the stickers on cars (and know in your heart that it reflects the price the car really should cost), and drive out with your new car, feeling satisfied that you got a good deal and the dealer made a small, fair profit.

Balderdash! Here's the real deal on many no-haggle dealers: They price their cars below MSRP (see Chapter 3) but still above dealer invoice, which, combined with their holdbacks or incentives, means they're making a few *thousand* dollars on each vehicle, when dealers who haggle may be making a few *hundred* dollars. And because you're relaxed and stress-free, you're much less resistant to the lure of add-on money-drainers: high financing rates, dealer prep costs, extended warranties, a low trade-in value for your existing vehicle, and so on. Although your experience will be pleasant, you'll likely pay thousands more than if you had been willing to haggle just a little!

In the same way, don't fall for the following trick many sales-people have been known to rely on. When they hear that you're shopping around, and you ask about their lowest price, some dealers will say, "Why don't you shop around and then come back here, and we'll beat your best price by $100." First, you have no guarantee that the dealer will remember or honor this offer, and second, you may have walked away from a good offer at another dealership because you thought you could beat it by $100 at the first dealer. If you do want to go back to the first dealership, get the agreement in writing before you leave to visit other dealerships.

Timing Your Approach

While doing your homework, steering clear of all the add-ons your dealer will try to throw your way, and standing your ground in negotiations can get you a great price on a new car, you may get an even better price by carefully timing your vehicle shopping.

End of the Model Year

The best time to buy a new car is as the new models are arriving. Many manufacturers release their new models in August or September, but late summer/early fall isn't new-model time for every manufacturer. Some new models come out in December, and others arrive in March. To find out when the new models will arrive at the dealerships you plan to target, call a few dealers in your area or contact the manufacturer directly (most manufacturers have e-mail and toll-free contact information on their Web sites).

After the new models have been on the lot for several weeks, make your move. Dealers want to get rid of their old models (which are still new cars, but have been on their lots for some time) to make room for the new models. You may not have a great selection of last year's cars to choose from, but if you're willing to make a few sacrifices, you'll likely negotiate a great price.

End of the Month

Dealers are often in competition with other dealers, both to meet their own sales goals and to generate the most sales of any dealer selling that brand of vehicle. To motivate dealers, manufacturers offer bonuses to dealers who sell the most cars in a given month. If you shop for a new vehicle as the month is wrapping up, your dealer may have an incentive to sell you a car—even if it isn't at the profit he or she would normally want.

Tax Time

Once a year, dealerships have to pay an inventory tax on the cars on their lots. While the due date varies from state to state, most states require automobile dealerships to count inventory in February, March, or April. As your local dealers approach this deadline, they'll bombard you with television ads about their tax sales. When you see those ads, you'll usually have until the end of the month to act. The closer to the deadline you get, the more willing each dealer will likely be to negotiate a low price in order not to pay inventory taxes on that vehicle.

Bringing a Friend—or Two!

When you approach one of your local dealers, knowing exactly the car you want, the price you're comfortable with, and how you plan to pay for your vehicle, bring a friend—or two or three! These friends don't have to speak or do any negotiating for you, they simply need to stay with you throughout your negotiations.

Car dealers use this approach all the time, but they think of it as "ganging-up on the customer," not as inviting a friend along. If you're alone at the dealership, a salesperson will greet you, try to find out what kind of car you're looking for and how serious you are about buying a car today, begin talking about the features of the car, and invite you to take a test drive. When you return from that test drive, he or she will ask you to sit down for a while to "find out what it'll take to get you into this car." If you show signs of interest in the price offered, the salesperson will stay with you until you make the decision to buy. But if you demonstrate that you know the dealer cost and holdbacks (see Chapter 3), and you're reaching an impasse about price, the salesperson will likely mention something about "having to talk to the manager." If you still aren't satisfied with the price after the salesperson shuttles back and forth to the manager a few times, the manager will enter the negotiations, and you'll find yourself facing two people, each talking quickly and trying to come up with offers you can't refuse. The manager will probably also act a bit annoyed, as though you're taking up his or her precious time.

But here's the rub: The whole thing's an act. Most salespeople don't have to ask their managers whether they can accept an offer that's at, just over, or just under invoice. Instead, they're trying to wear you down, making you embarrassed that you're causing such a hassle over a few hundred dollars.

This is where your friends come in. As the salesperson and manager exchange exacerbated looks and sigh heavily, you do the same. Use your friend to bounce around the offers you get: "$18,100—that's still just too much. I don't think this is going to work out today." If your salespeople are truly at their lower limit, they'll let this sort of conversation go on until you and your friend leave the dealership. But if they have a few more dollars of wiggle room, they'll quickly counteroffer.

Whatever the dealer offers you—an extended warranty at a price you can't afford to give up or a dealer-installed stereo that's a once-in-a-lifetime deal—bounce the idea off your friends. Say things to your friend like, "I definitely can't afford that extended warranty if it's over $400" or "I know Aunt Betty will buy my old car for $3,500, so I don't think I'll trade it in today," giving the dealer time to absorb your answer and make a counteroffer, if possible.

Standing Your Ground— But Giving a Little

Before going to a dealership, make hard and fast decisions about how much you can pay, whether you're willing to lease or buy a used car, and which options—if any—you're willing to purchase. Have these decisions clear in your mind and don't go to a dealership until you know you won't waver on any of these issues.

Ultimately, you may have to walk away from the dealership empty-handed if you're not able to get the car you want at the price you want, but that's a basic rule of any negotiation. If you're unwilling to walk away, you're probably unwilling to work patiently and diligently for the best price, and you'll end up being talked into a higher price or more options than you wanted in the first place.

Do, however, leave a cushion in your offer. If you know you can't go above $18,000, don't offer $18,000 to begin with. Instead offer $17,700 and allow yourself to "give in" that last $300.

Walking Away

If negations aren't going the way you'd hope, chalk up your time at the dealership to great experience, and then head home. If you aren't willing to walk away at any time, you'll likely be talked into making a decision that you'll regret. If you have the slightest twinge of doubt about the direction the negotiations are going, be prepared to walk away without anger or frustration. Just tell the dealer, "Thanks so much for your time. I'll come back on another day." Be wary of any dealer who forces you to make a decision on the spot or tells you that a particular price will expire that day or within a few hours.

Negotiating Online

The very easiest way to "negotiate" is to not negotiate at all but to gather quotes from dealers within a 100- or 200-mile radius of your home—all on the Internet—and then choose the lowest price. I recently visited several new-vehicle Web sites to gather quotes for a new car, and I was thrilled with the process.

A few elements of the process were a little unsettling, however. I sent out over twenty requests for quotes in a 200-mile radius of my home and received only four back. Two dealers gave me prices that were about halfway between the MRSP and the dealer invoice costs. A third dealer didn't understand the process at all and tried to sell me on the fantastic service that his dealership could offer—a dealership that was 150 miles from my home. In my e-mail reply, I explained that service was irrelevant to me, because I would probably never live anywhere near his dealership. His prices were also quite high. A fourth dealer, however, immediately wrote back with an offer than was about $250 *less* than invoice—right around the price I had originally hoped for. I verified with this dealer, who is located about 90 miles from my home, what was included in that price. I also e-mailed the dealers that didn't win my business (letting them know about the low price I was offered) to thank them for their time and effort.

To get new-car prices and quotes from dealers, check out the following new-car Web sites.

- Autobytel: *www.autobytel.com*
- Autoweb: *www.autoweb.com*

- CarsDirect: *carsdirect.com*
- CarSmart: *www.carsmart.com*
- Stoneage: *www.stoneage.com*
- Vehicles-on-Line: *www.vehiclesonline.com*

If you use Autobytel, choose the e-mail response option instead of the phone response. Having a dealer call you can be unnerving, because he or she will still be using professional negotiation skills to feel out your parameters before making you an offer. The anonymity of e-mail—and the fact that you get time to quietly read and compose e-mail messages—makes for a much more low-key negotiation process.

Try to keep an open mind about shopping on the Internet. Recent studies have shown that a large number of MSRP and invoice prices listed online are slightly skewed. If a dealer angrily insists that you're working with the wrong MSRP and invoice price, ask him to show you where your mistake is, and then get back to negotiations.

chapter six

The Finer Points of Negotiating a Lease

If you have carefully considered your options and decided that leasing a car is for you, Chapter 5 has probably been helpful to you in giving you general advice on how to negotiate with car dealers. But leasing a car is no easy task—even seasoned professionals have trouble understanding the finer points of leases.

Getting into a lease is pretty easy from a dealer's perspective: You can be in and out of a dealership with a lease in less than an hour. You, however, should spend as much time researching and planning your lease as you would a purchase. This chapter will cover all you need to know in order to negotiate a leasing deal that will make sense for you, and that you'll be comfortable with.

Negotiate the Purchase Price First

Approach a lease as though you're going to buy the vehicle. Using the strategies provided in Chapter 3, come up with a purchase price you think is appropriate, and see if you can get the dealer to agree to it. Only at that point do you want to reveal that you're planning to lease the vehicle, instead of buying it. You can then use the purchase price you have agreed upon with the dealer to calculate the adjusted capitalized cost—the total lease amount, excluding any rebates, down payments, or trade-in allowances.

Negotiate the Down Payment and Security Deposit

A lease that's advertised a "zero down payment" will still require cash up-front in the form of a security deposit (usually one month's payment, plus a small processing fee), the first month's payment, a $250 to $500 bank fee (negotiate for $250), and a $50 to $100 documentation/preparation fee. That's a lot of cash for "zero down payment."

Many lessors will also try to talk you into opting for a higher down payment to lower your monthly payments. Keep in mind that your down payment (also called your capitalized cost or capitalized cost reduction) is not reducing the price of the vehicle—it's only changing when you pay the amount required to lease the car. You can pay a large down payment up front to lower your monthly payments, or make a small or no down payment up front and make high monthly payments. In addition, if you should get into an accident and total the vehicle, your down payment would be lost forever. Chances are, you can use the couple thousand dollars in cash right now and make higher monthly payments as you go along, so opt for a low (or no) down payment.

Security deposits are usually not negotiable, but it can't hurt to try. Balk at any security deposit that's much higher than one month's payment. (Keep in mind, though, that you will get your security deposit back at the end of your lease contract.)

Negotiate the Length of the Lease

The longer the length of your lease, the more money you're going to put into the vehicle in the form of major tune-ups and new tires. Because you won't own the car at the end of the lease contract, that money will have been wasted. Instead, opt for the shortest contract length you can afford—twenty-four, thirty, or (at most) thirty-six months—and make sure the vehicle warranty will be in effect the entire time you're leasing the vehicle.

If you can't afford the monthly payments for a lease of these lengths, consider your other options: lease a less-expensive vehicle, buy the vehicle and spread the payments out over a longer period but own the vehicle at the end of the contract, or buy a used version of the same vehicle.

Negotiate the Residual Value and Money Factor

The residual value is the theoretical value of the vehicle at the end of the lease contract. If this number is too low, your monthly payments will be too high. If the residual value is too high and you want to purchase the vehicle at the end of the lease, you'll pay too much to purchase the vehicle at that time. If you have to choose, opt for a high residual that will result in low monthly payments. If you can't renegotiate the residual value at the end of the lease contract, simply walk away from the deal and don't consider purchasing your leased vehicle.

Usually, the dealership or finance company tells you the residual value of the car you're leasing, and you must either accept that number or walk away from the deal. You can, however, purchase a leasing software program that will give you the residual value of any car you're considering and estimate your other leasing costs. These programs also spot hidden fees that you may not otherwise notice. Several such programs can be purchased online; they are generally priced at around $100. To find the latest versions of leasing software, log on to a search engine and type in "leasing software."

Because it is important to know the residual value of a vehicle you plan to lease, opt for a closed-end lease instead of an open-ended one—pen-ended leases leave the residual value to be determined at the end of the lease contract.

Finally, you want your money factor (or lease rate) to be as low as possible. Think of the money factor as a leasing equivalent to financing rate. In fact, you can convert a money factor to an annual percentage rate (APR) by multiplying the money factor by 2400. For example, a money factor of 0.00375 is equivalent to 9 percent APR. Ask your dealer to shop around with several leasing agents and let you know what the money factors are for each company. Then choose the lowest rate.

Negotiate the Annual Mileage Allotment

You want to negotiate the highest number of miles per year that you can get. Most leases allow from 12,000 to 15,000, so you want to be on the high side of that range. Also negotiate the per-mile charge that you'll incur if you exceed your mileage allotment.

These charges range from ten cents a mile (which is reasonable) to an exorbitantly high twenty-five cents per mile. You want the lowest per-mile charge you can get. Also see whether you can negotiate for a refund if you don't use all of the allotted miles or whether you can "buy" extra miles at the beginning of your contract for less than you would pay in penalty fees for exceeding the mileage.

You also want to make sure you fully understand the wear and tear that's allowed versus wear and tear that's excessive. If you're hard on your car—say, for example, you ride with your dogs and they have sharp claws or you regularly spill coffee on the front seats—you'll want to either negotiate for more allowable wear and tear terms, or consider buying instead of leasing.

Negotiate Early-Termination Fees and Subleasing Options

Should you change your mind and want to turn your vehicle in earlier than you originally thought, you don't want to be charged an arm and a leg. While you're negotiating, see how low you can get your early-termination fee. Ideally, your contract will state that you can terminate the lease without incurring a penalty.

When early-termination fees are excessive, some people opt for subleasing instead. Subleasing a car is just like subleasing an apartment: Someone else (a sublessee) starts driving the leased vehicle and takes over the monthly lease payments for you. Often, people with poor credit records are enthusiastic about subleasing, because they see it as an opportunity to make a series of monthly payments and improve their credit records. The original lease contract, however, is rarely changed to reflect the name of the sublessee, so the sublessee does not establish a better credit record. In addition, the original lessee runs the risk of having the sublessee default on the payments, thus damaging the lessee's own credit record and losing possession of the vehicle. This is a bad situation for everyone. Before you lease a vehicle, discuss the possibility of subleasing with your leasing agent. If you find out that subleasing is not allowed, don't do it—not even for a good friend or family member. You may wind up with no car and a credit report that doesn't allow you to buy or lease another.

Negotiate Other Fees and Conditions

Don't pay upfront acquisition fees or lease-end disposal or disposition fees. You can find dealers who won't charge these fees, so walk away if you're told you must pay them.

Do try to include an option to buy your car into your contract, but don't lock into buying. You want an option to buy written in, but you also want to be able to walk away and not buy without penalty.

Register and Insure Your Leased Car

You have to register a leased car just like a car you own, but the car must be registered in the name of the leasing company, with you as the co-owner. This probably means that you can't transfer the registration from your current vehicle, so registration may be a bit tricky. Ask your dealer or leasing agent to help.

In addition to getting standard insurance for your vehicle, pay for gap insurance that covers the depreciation that new vehicles suffer in the first few weeks they're driven off the lot. If you should be in an accident or your vehicle is stolen, the gap insurance plus your regular insurance will cover the entire cost of the vehicle. Without gap insurance, you could be stuck paying the difference between the purchase price and the much-lower current value of the vehicle.

Carefully Read and Sign All Documents

For every word or calculation you don't understand, ask to have it explained. The documents you sign should match the verbal agreements you've previously made. Don't sign anything that you don't understand—it could cost you dearly at the end of the lease contract.

chapter seven

Taking the Plunge— Buying a Car

After you've officially decided that you want to purchase a new car—and not lease one (see Chapter 4 for the pros and cons of both)—you have to actually go out and buy it. You basically have three options: buying through the Internet, at a dealer's showroom, or at a megastore. In addition, if you're buying a used car, you can use all three of these options and also scan the classified ads for vehicles sold by car owners.

Buying a New or Used Car Through the Internet

The easiest way to get quotes from various dealers is to use the Internet, but that option can make for a difficult delivery of your vehicle, which involves inspecting the vehicle, handing over money, and signing paperwork. To simplify matters, stick to your neck of the woods when seeking quotes for vehicles—I recommend not straying more than 200 miles from home in any direction. That way, you'll have to drive three and a half hours each way, at most, which you can do in a day. Dealers can also have your car delivered to you for an additional price. Handling the paperwork in those situations can be a little tricky, however.

I recommend the following sites for obtaining quotes in a particular geographic area (also see "Negotiating Online" in Chapter 5):

- CarsDirect: *carsdirect.com*
- Autoweb: *www.autoweb.com*
- CarSmart: *www.carsmart.com*
- Stoneage: *www.stoneage.com*
- Vehicles-on-Line: *www.vehiclesonline.com*
- Autobytel: *www.autobytel.com*

Buying a New or Used Car at a Dealer's Showroom

The thought of buying a car at a dealer's showroom leaves me cold. Although this old routine feels like the way car-buying should be, I'm not a fan of tough negotiations, and buying a car the old-fashioned way is becoming less and less appealing.

A dealer's showroom is most helpful, however, when you're unsure which model you're particularly interested in. You can test-drive a number of vehicles on your list, compare MSRPs, and also look at used cars before making a final decision about which car you want to purchase.

If you do decide to go through a live negotiating process (as opposed to getting quotes on the Internet to buy a car), keep the negotiating tips in Chapter 5 fresh in your mind.

Buying a New or Used Car at a Megastore

Megastores are huge Disneyland-sized car dealerships that may sell vehicles from twenty different manufacturers under one roof. These stores are ideal for getting ideas—and for making good deals on inexpensive, high-volume vehicles. Even if you're completely unsure which make, model, or even vehicle category you're interested in, as long as you approach your first time at a megastore as a learning opportunity, you may get to examine, kick the tires of, and test-drive dozens of cars in one day, at one location.

Most moderate-to-large cities have one megastore. If your town doesn't have one, consider taking a one-day trip to the nearest big city to take a peek at all the options available to you. You'll surely find something you like.

After you've selected a vehicle, if you like in-person negotiations, approach the megastore about its lowest possible prices. If the prices are too high, negotiate or walk away.

Buying a Used Car from the Classified Ads

Before buying a car from a classified ad, be sure to review the pros and cons of buying a used car in Chapter 2. Always insist on seeing all maintenance records for any used car you're considering purchasing, and never purchase a vehicle until you've had a mechanic review it for you. You can put a deposit on the car to hold it, but write "Refundable deposit contingent on mechanic's review" in the memo portion of the check.

chapter eight

Financing Your Vehicle

Cars are expensive toys, so before you set foot in the high-pressure vehicle sales world of your nearest dealership, narrow your financing options to just two or three possibilities. Before you decide, look at all the options—local financial institutions, financial arms of vehicle manufacturers (who may be offering a low finance rate as an incentive to buy their products), Internet financing, and so on. This chapter helps you sort through the options.

Accepting Dealer Financing

Getting financing through your dealer is by far the cleanest, simplest way to finance a vehicle. You bring in your cash down payment, and an hour or so later, you drive away in your new car.

There is, however, one problem with using your dealer for financing: Unless you have a clear idea of the prevailing finance rates for new cars, your dealer may charge you from ½ to 2 percent higher than his or her normal rate, and pocket the difference to make up for the low price you paid for your new vehicle. To guard against this, keep a small notebook or pad of paper with you as you shop for your new car. In that notebook, keep a record of all the prevailing finance rates in your town and on the Internet.

Getting a Loan at Your Local Bank or Credit Union

Your local bank or credit union is a great place to shop for a low finance rate. With a few quick phone calls, you can determine which bank offers the best rates, and then go with the lowest rate or with the bank with the most convenient locations, hours, and other intangibles.

Finding Financing on the Internet

Finding financing on the Internet is a breeze, and you can check ever-changing interest rates as often as you like. Often, you get a response to your loan application in minutes.

Consider using the following Internet financing sources:

- e-Loan: *www.eloan.com*
- PeopleFirst.com: *www.peoplefirst.com*
- AutoAgent: *www.autoagent.com*

Keep in mind that every time you apply for a loan online, it shows up on your credit report. You don't want to have an excessive number of loan applications on your record, even if you never leave your comfy chair to complete the applications.

Taking Advantage of Finance-Rate Specials

When a vehicle manufacturer offers a low finance rate that you don't think you can get anywhere else, contact the manufacturer (not the dealer) directly to see how you can get preapproved for a loan. This way, by the time you walk into the dealership or megastore, your loan will already be approved, and you don't have to worry about haggling over finance rates and lengths of contracts with your salesperson. And if you decide to purchase a new car via the Internet, your financing will have already been secured, leaving less paperwork for the delivery day.

Trading In a Vehicle

I advise against using your old vehicle for a trade-in. First, you may not receive a very fair price on the vehicle you're trading in, especially if you were tough in your negotiations about the price of your new car. The dealer may see your trade-in as an opportunity to make up for the money he or she lost to your new-car negotiation skills. Second, dealers have to make money on their used cars, so they will pay you less than you would be able to get from an individual buyer. Then, they'll mark the car up a few thousand dollars to see how much of a profit they can make on it.

My philosophy is this: If someone is willing to buy your old car for $2,000 more than you were paid for it by the dealer, why not try to find that person instead of selling your old car to the dealership? You may be $2,000 richer in the process.

Paying Cash

Paying cash is probably the simplest, most rewarding way you can buy a vehicle, but keep in mind that if interest rates fall low enough (like, say, zero percent), you'll be able to save money by financing your vehicle and investing your down payment.

chapter nine

Preserving Your Car's Resale Value

If you plan to lease a car and not purchase it at the end of your lease contract, you can ignore this chapter completely. But if you're buying a car and think you'll want to trade it in three years from now, are buying a car that you plan to keep for fifteen years, or are leasing a car that you think you may want to purchase when your lease agreement expires, this chapter can help you preserve your car's resale value.

Unlike a house, a car depreciates—that is, it loses value—with time. In fact, a car loses 30 to 50 percent of its value in the first three, four, or five years you own it. The longer you keep a car, however, the less you feel the sting of depreciation, because this rate slows down considerably after five years. In the same way, depreciation takes less of a toll if you buy a used vehicle, because the car will already have lost much of its value before you purchased it.

This chapter will show you the steps that you can take to

preserve your vehicle's resale value from the moment you first begin driving it—and even earlier!

Buy a Popular Vehicle

If you're interested in minimizing your car's depreciation, buy a car that a lot of other people are buying. This won't make you stand out on the crowded road, but that's the point: If few people want to buy a vehicle when it's new, they won't want to buy it (or pay very much for it) when it's used.

Mid-sized sedans—especially the Toyota Camry, Honda Accord, and Ford Taurus—have been consistently popular for years. Minivans, especially the Dodge Caravan and the Honda Odyssey, are nearly always well liked. The Honda Civic has been in style for years, and Ford Focus, the successor to the Ford Escort, is wildly popular right now. Among pickup trucks, the Ford F-Series, Chevrolet Silverado, and Ford Ranger are selling well, and if you're in the market for an SUV, the Ford Explorer and Jeep Grand Cherokee are hot commodities. Among station wagons, the Subaru Outback is quite popular.

There is a down side to buying popular vehicles: They're more likely to be targeted by car thieves because the parts command top dollar from unscrupulous body and repair shops. If you purchase a popular vehicle, consider also installing a vehicle-security system—but don't get it from your dealer! Instead, have a system installed after you purchase the car, at a reputable shop.

Buy a Popular Color

If you buy a lime-green or purple car, you may have trouble selling it, which means your resale value will be lower. Always choose classic colors over trendy ones, but keep in mind that dark colors tend to show nicks and scratches more readily than light colors, and are also more popular with car thieves.

Choose Your Options Carefully

Chapter 3 discusses ways you can save money when you purchase a vehicle, and one way is to avoid dealer-installed and manufacturer options that you don't need. Heeding this advice can also improve your resale value, because most people aren't interested in paying for those options—alloy wheels, ground effects and other aerodynamic kits, masks, racing stripes, and so on—in a used vehicle. Do, however, opt for air conditioning (the most popular option), an automatic transmission, and (if you can afford them) cruise control and a sunroof. Another popular feature is a stereo system (which can be purchased at several online as well as bricks-and-mortar electronics stores).

Also match your options to the vehicle category. A compact car doesn't require all the bells and whistles that a luxury car would have. In a mid-priced sedan, used-car buyers are looking for power door locks, power windows, and high-quality stereo systems. Sports car owners tend to prefer manual transmissions.

Review a Potential Vehicle's Expected Resale Value

Perhaps the most obvious way to preserve the resale value of your car is to buy a new car that tends to have good resale value. Sounds like circular logic, doesn't it? Really, it's not. Before purchasing a vehicle, look at the value of used vehicles of the same make and model that are three, five, and ten years old. Compare that resale value to the used-car cost of other cars you're considering, and choose the vehicle that will depreciate the least (the one with the highest potential resale value). Although auto manufacturers often suggest to you that their vehicles are more affordable than others on the market because they offer the same (or more) interior space, warranty, and comfort at a lower price, those lower-priced models often lose their resale value more quickly than the cars they're compared to.

To find out the potential resale value of a vehicle, visit the Kelley Blue Book Web site at *www.kbb.com.* You can also use the IntelliChoice awards *(www.intellichoice.com),* and then click on "Best Values" to help you determine potential resale value of a particular car. IntelliChoice rates cars based on a variety of factors—purchase price, depreciation (which is the potential resale value), maintenance, and so on—to determine which cars will have the best values over the next five years. Although you won't be looking solely at resale value, the rating system that IntelliChoice uses can be extremely helpful when choosing your next vehicle.

Avoid buying a vehicle the first year it's released, because you have no way of knowing what its potential resale value will be. When I was a semester away from graduating from college, I made a bad decision to purchase a new car on impulse. I won't share the name of the manufacturer, but I didn't do any homework and walked into the dealership like a lamb led to slaughter. The salesperson noticed my interest in one of the vehicles on the showroom floor and immediately went to work on me. Now, this was one of those compact cars that was fully loaded with a sunroof, stereo system, power everything, alloy wheels, and—I can hardly believe this was an attraction to me—ground effects on the front, back, and both sides (these are colored, molded plastic pieces that fit along the base of the car and give it the race-car look). The dealer opened the showroom doors, and I took a test-drive along with the salesperson, who told me that even though this model was in its first year and few people were familiar with this manufacturer who was new to the American car market, he was positive that this car would end up having a better resale value than any other car on the road. I bought it (both the line and the car), paid top dollar for it (haggling on the purchase price but then not even blinking at the low price they offered me for my trade-in), and could almost see the car depreciating before my eyes. Who wants a used, souped-up compact car from an unknown manufacturer? Suffice it to say that when I could no longer stand to drive the car a moment longer—about six years later—I actually had to *pay* a $300 disposal fee to get rid of it. It had absolutely no—zero, zippo, nada—resale value.

Buy a Vehicle with Good Bumpers

Vehicles generally come with one of three types of bumpers, as follows:

- The best-looking vehicles have bumpers on the front and back (and, perhaps, also on the sides) of the vehicle, and these bumpers match the paint color. The problem is that when you actually hit something with these bumpers (or when something, like a shopping cart, hits you), the bumpers crack or dent, making your car less attractive.
- Other cars have black-colored bumpers on the front, back, and sides, but these bumpers are usually made from a formed plastic. While these bumpers can usually withstand a five-mile-per-hour fender-bender, a more substantial collision—even with a shopping cart winging its way through a parking lot on a windy day—will usually result in dings and dents.

- A few cars still have dense rubber bumpers that wrap around the car. While these bumpers aren't terribly attractive, if you can find a popular car with rubber bumpers, you're going to emerge with a less dented and dinged vehicle than you would with other bumpers.

I was once driving down a busy six-lane road—in my sedan with wrap-around rubber bumpers—when a woman trying to swat an insect in her car moved out of her lane and into mine, thumping my car on the right side. We both pulled over to the side of the road, and when I got out, I saw that her left side (bumperless) was dented pretty badly. When I checked my car, I couldn't find a scratch on it. Although we were traveling at fifty miles per hour, my rubber bumpers had bounced her car off of mine without removing even a scrape of paint. I've been sold on rubber bumpers ever since.

Touch Up the Exterior

When you purchase a vehicle (new or used), take a trip to the service counter of your local dealer and ask for a bottle of touch-up paint. You'll pay close to $10 for a bottle that's about the size of nail polish, but this investment will pay off handsomely.

For the remainder of the time you own your vehicle, every time you wash it, check the exterior for spots of missing paint. By carefully applying a tiny amount of touch-up paint to each spot, you'll reduce the risk of rust damage.

Drive Carefully

Driving carefully means two things: driving safely and taking it easy on your car.

Driving safely makes sense: If you can avoid getting into accidents, your vehicle will look and drive more like new. You can't always avoid accidents, but do be on the lookout for other drivers. To improve your reaction time, don't eat, talk on a cell phone, fiddle with the stereo system, or change CDs while driving. When driving conditions worsen—such as during a severe rainstorm or when traffic increases at rush hour—you may also want to refrain from listening to the radio and conversing with passengers. You'll be able to better concentrate on the road.

If you are in an accident, get any damage repaired right away. You shouldn't put off repairs because you don't want to pay your deductible, or want to spend a claim check from an insurance company on a vacation or new clothes. If you got into an auto accident, try to restore your vehicle to a like-new condition.

Being easy on your car may be even more difficult than driving safely. Ever wonder why used cars owned by little old ladies are so popular? Because it's hard to imagine them driving on a cold engine, revving up the engine, or making a lot of stops and starts. Allow plenty of time for your car to warm up. If you can keep your vehicle in a garage, you won't need to warm it up at all—simply drive under fifty or fifty-five miles per hour for the first five minutes of your trip. If your vehicle is parked on your driveway or a parking lot on a cold day, let the motor run for a few minutes before driving. When you start driving, stay under fifty-five miles per hour for a few minutes.

In the same way, don't slam on your brakes (instead, anticipate stops and slow down well in advance) or floor the gas pedal after stoplights and stop signs (accelerate gradually, instead).

You also don't want to regularly take short trips in your vehicle. If you live two miles from work, you'll wreak havoc on your vehicle by making ten two-mile trips per week (that's 500 two-mile trips per year!) because your vehicle will never get a

chance to warm up before you turn it off again. Instead, walk or
bike to work or carpool with a coworker. In the same way, instead
of driving from one end of a shopping center to another to visit
two stores there, park your car at one location, walk to the other,
and walk back again. It's a healthy idea—both for your car's
engine and for you.

Keep Your Mileage Down

Ten years ago, used cars with over 90,000 or 100,000 miles were
considered a risky purchase. But with manufacturers building
vehicles to last longer—and offering warranties to back up their
claims that they really will last that long—people are keeping
their cars longer and feeling confident that they'll last. The
average age of vehicles on the road today is about ten years, so by
driving even 12,000 miles per year, the average car will have seen
120,000 miles.

Still, mileage is a major factor in a vehicle's resale value, and
used-car shoppers would rather buy a low-mileage car than a
high-mileage one. You can reduce your mileage by walking or
riding a bike on short errands, moving closer to work, and renting
a vehicle for long roadtrips.

Take Care of the Interior

A used vehicle isn't going to still have that new-car smell by the
time you go to sell it, but you can keep the interior looking new
throughout the life of the vehicle. Be especially careful with food
in your car—just as certain foods can stain your sofa, you could
be looking at that ketchup stain on the driver's seat for the next
ten years. Seat covers are always a good idea. If you have a dog,
cover the seats with a sheet or towel to keep mud from caking on

the upholstery. Trim your dog's nails, too, so that they don't damage the fabric.

To keep your upholstery from fading and the steering wheel from cracking, use a dashboard cover to block the sun. These run the gamut from ultra-sophisticated styles that look like they belong on the space shuttle to basic, fold-up cardboard inserts that you can get at Wal-Mart. Whatever you choose, insert one in both your front and rear windows any time your car will be exposed to the sun for more than thirty minutes or so.

Before you sell your car, be sure to get it detailed—a fancy word that just means thoroughly washed, inside and out. For about $100, detailers will vacuum the carpets, deep-clean the upholstery, dust and wash the dashboard and all crevices where crumbs collect, and wash the windows (inside and out). They'll also wash the exterior of your car, including the tires.

No Smoking in Your Car

With the number of nonsmokers growing rapidly in the United States, your chances of finding a smoker when you try to sell your vehicle are pretty low. Nonsmokers don't want to smell smoke when they drive, and the smell of smoke is nearly impossible to get out of carpeting and upholstery, so if you want to maximize your resale value, don't smoke in your car.

Don't Forget Regular Maintenance Work

An oil change consists of replacing the oil, replacing the oil filter, topping off all fluids in the vehicle, inspecting for fluid leaks, and checking/changing the tire pressure. They're pretty cheap ($20 to $25) and fast (ten to thirty minutes). Get an oil change every 3,000 miles, and you'll save a tremendous amount of wear and tear on your vehicle. (Many people recommend an oil change every 5,000 or 7,500 miles, but given how little each oil change costs, you're better off going with every 3,000.) Whenever you get an oil change, ask to have the air filter replaced, too. Every two oil changes, ask to have the fuel filter (sometimes called the gas filter) replaced.

When replacing major parts (such as during a tune-up or for a major repair), make sure the parts were produced by your car's manufacturer—so if you're driving a General Motors car, use genuine GM parts. This probably means you'll have to have your vehicle serviced at a dealer instead of an independent service station, but as a result, you'll be using parts that are made to fit the exact specifications of your vehicle.

For the first 20,000 miles, get your vehicle serviced (preferably at your dealership) every 5,000 miles. After 20,000 miles, you can wait until 30,000 miles for a major tune-up and inspection. After 30,000 miles, get a minor tune-up and inspection every 15,000 miles and a major tune-up and inspection every 30,000. Your dealer will know what to check and replace at these tune-ups. At 90,000 miles, you'll also want to replace all your belts, which can be expensive. These inspections and tune-ups aren't cheap (the major ones cost a few hundred dollars), but your car will run so smoothly that your resale value will soar.

Keep Track of Your Service Records

Remember to keep good records—including receipts—for all your vehicle maintenance. No one will believe you when you tell them that you opted for oil changes every 3,000 miles and serviced your car every 15,000 miles. Proven records of oil changes, tire replacement, and regular service, however, will make your car more valuable when you sell it.

chapter ten

Becoming a Car Buff—Auto Shows and Events

By the time you get to this chapter, you should have every-thing you need to know in order to buy or lease the car you want for the price you are willing to pay. But perhaps you want more—you like cars, like talking about them, like to visit auto shows, car museums, and auto races. This chapter will give you a brief over-look of what is out there in the world of cars.

Auto shows, where new vehicles, renovated models, and futuristic concept cars are displayed and demonstrated, can be great fun for an entire family. To find up-to-date information about the major American and international auto shows, check out *www.edmunds.com.*

Other auto events include classic car shows, museums, and auto races—another way to keep cars and trucks in your blood. Prices vary from about $10 for a day at an auto show to $100 for a highbrow classic car show or race.

U.S. Auto Shows

The four U.S. international auto shows draw more than a million visitors each, and smaller new-car shows draw tens of thousands to major cities around the country.

North American International Auto Show (NAIAS)— Cobo Hall, Detroit, Michigan (mid-January)

The NAIAS in Detroit is the *crème de la crème* of auto shows. (Clearly, having grown up in the Motor City hasn't biased my thinking.) Every publication in the world sends a representative to this show, held each year in chilly January, for the earliest look at concept cars and new models, plus lots of free giveaways and a host of brochures and catalogs. While in town, stop in for a Red Wings hockey game at Joe Louis Arena next door.

Greater Los Angeles Auto Show—Los Angeles, California (early January)

Also held in January, the Greater Los Angeles Auto Show is a warm-weather rival to NAIAS. This shows isn't as large—nor anywhere as flashy—as the show in Detroit, but if you live on the west coast and want to see a major auto show, the LA show is a good choice.

New York International Auto Show—Javits Center, New York, New York (mid-April)

Every major manufacturer presents vehicles at the New York International Auto Show, now over 100 years strong. Like other shows, you get to see amazing concept cars and all of the new models to come out the following year. The major advantage to attending the New York show is that it's in New York, which is always worth a visit.

Chicago Auto Show—McCormick Plaza South, Chicago, Illinois (mid-February)

The Chicago Auto Show has what most other auto shows offer—peeks at new models and demonstrations of concept cars that may never make it to full production. But this show also offers the best preview of American-made and foreign trucks that will be on the market shortly.

Other New-Car Shows

Most major cities host a new-car auto show each spring or summer to unveil the new models and model updates. To find a show in your area, search the Internet under "auto show" and the name of your city or visit *Motor Trend* magazine's most current list of auto shows at *www.motortrend.com.*

Specialty Equipment Market Association (SEMA) Show—Las Vegas, Nevada (early November)

While the SEMA show does include some vehicle displays and demonstrations, the focus of this show is on aftermarket auto components. You have to be a pretty big car buff to enjoy this one.

International Auto Shows

Attending an auto show in Europe places you among the elite auto show buffs—and it's a good excuse to visit Europe in the process. The following are the three largest:

- **Frankfurt Internationale Automobil-Ausstellung:** Held at the Messe Frankfurt Convention Center in Frankfurt, Germany, in mid-September, the Frankfurt Motor Show competes each year with the Paris show as the largest in Europe.

- **Paris Mondail de L'Automobile:** Held in September, the Paris Auto Show in Paris, France, gives you an opportunity to visit one of the great European cities as you peruse the latest models and concept cars.
- **Geneva Auto Show:** This diverse and fairly low-key show is held in early March in Geneva, Switzerland, near Lake Geneva and the Alps.

Vintage Vehicle Shows and Races

Vintage vehicles are another name for classic cars, but whereas classic cars refer to any older car that's in good condition, vintage vehicles are older vehicles that are pristine, incredibly expensive, and stunningly beautiful. The term *Concours d'Elegance* means "gathering of elegance," a car show to which only the finest vintage vehicles are invited. These vehicles are often museum pieces that are brought out only for these events. From Bentleys and Pierce-Arrows to Studebakers and Rolls Royces, every *Concours d'Elegance* features premiere classic cars from both the U.S. and overseas. Occasionally, these cars even get together for races.

The following lists a few of the premiere events across the country; for a more thorough listing, search for "Concours D'Elegance" on any Internet search engine.

- **Meadow Brook Concours d'Elegance:** Rochester, Michigan (early August). Held at the former home of automotive baroness Matilda Dodge Wilson, the *Concours d'Elegance* at Meadow Brook Hall is worth the trip. Many of the cars displayed are from the heyday of automobiles—the 1930s. While you're at the show, take the tour of Meadow Brook Hall, one of the most spectacular mansions in the country. See the event's Web site at *www.mbhconcours.org*.

- **Concours d'Elegance of the Eastern United States:** Bethlehem, Pennsylvania (mid-June). This event features a number of categories, including original cars (which have had little or no restoration work but still meet the vehicle quality requirements), sports cars, and 1950s muscle cars. Visit *www.concourseast.org* for more information.
- **Monterey Historic Races:** Monterey peninsula, California (third weekend in August). Planned in conjunction with the Pebble Beach *Concours d'Elegance*, an extraordinary event that features cars from as far back as the turn of the century, and the *Concorso Italiano*, which celebrates Italian automotive genius, the Monterey Historic Races takes you back to the glory days of race car driving—you can watch Bentlys and Studebakers take to an eleven-turn track. Click on *www.pebblebeach concours.net* for details.

Museums

Car and truck museums are another great way to witness the beauty of automotive technology. Most set a reasonable entry fee, so the entire family can spend a day surrounded by these fascinating machines. Some of the most prominent are listed here.

- **Antique Automobile Club Of America (AACA):** Hershey, Pennsylvania. The AACA will soon open a museum dedicated to preserving classic cars and memorabilia. Visit *www.aaca.org* for more information.
- **The Art Car Museum:** Houston, Texas. This unique museum features art that was created from automobiles: the Wrought Iron VW Bug, for example. Visit *www.art carmuseum.com* for more information.

- **The Auburn-Cord-Duesenberg Museum:** Auburn, Indiana. Located at the headquarters of the now-defunct Auburn Automobile Company, this museum displays Auburns, Cords, Duesenbergs, Packards, Cadillacs, Rolls Royces, and other exquisitely preserved vintage cars. Visit *www.clearlake.com/auburn/acd.htm* for more information.
- **Blackhawk Automotive Museum:** Danville, California. The Blackhawk Museum features a 100-car exhibition that represents four eras of the automobile. Visit *www.blackhawkauto.org* for more information.
- **Harold E. LeMay Museum:** Tacoma, Washington. The *Guinness Book of Records* recognizes Harold LeMay's private collection as the largest in the world. View vintage vehicles, ambulances, fire trucks, and more. Visit *www.lemaymuseum.org* for more information.
- **Hays Antique Truck Museum:** Woodland, California. This museum offers the largest collection of antique trucks in the nation. Manufacturers include Breeding, Fageol, Freightliner, Mack, Oshkosh, Peterbilt, and Sterling. Visit *www.truckmuseum.org* for more information.
- **Henry Ford Museum and Greenfield Village:** Dearborn, Michigan. The Henry Ford Museum and Greenfield Village is the largest indoor/outdoor museum in North America. You'll find an amazing exhibition of the evolution of transportation, manufacturing, and inventions. Definitely worth the trip, especially with kids. Visit *www.hfmgv.org/museum* for more information.
- **The Museum of Automobile History:** Syracuse, New York. Follow the progress of car manufacturing from early attempts in the late 1770s to the cars of today. Visit *www.autolit.com/museum/index.htm* for more information.
- **The National Corvette Museum:** Bowling Green, Kentucky. This museum houses nothing but Corvettes. If

you're a fan of these sports cars, this museum may seem too good to be true. Visit *www.corvettemuseum.com* for more information.

- **The Petersen Automotive Museum:** Los Angeles, California. The Petersen Museum features over 100 years of automobiles. On the third floor, be sure to stop by the Discovery Center, which features hands-on activities that explore basic engineering principles that apply to automobiles. Visit *www.petersen.org* for more information.

- **Sarasota Car Museum:** Sarasota, Florida. This third-oldest automobile museum in the United States strives to entertain and educate patrons about how automobiles have impacted and benefited American culture. Visit *www.sarasotacarmuseum.org* for more information.

- **S. Ray Miller Auto Museum:** Elkhart, Indiana. *Car Collector* magazine voted the Miller Museum as one of the ten best small auto museums in the nation. Here, you'll find models from Auburn, Avanti, Cord, Corvette, Duesenberg, Elcar, Marmon Sixteen, Packard, Reo Royale, Ruxton, Sterling, Studebaker, and Stutz. Visit *www.millerautomuseum.org* for more information.

- **The Sloan Museum:** Flint, Michigan. The Sloan Museum honors Alfred P. Sloan, General Motors' first president, with exhibits of historic automobiles and information on General Motors' rise to power. Visit *www.ipl.org/exhibit/sloan/sloan-info.html* for more information.

- **Studebaker National Museum:** South Bend, Indiana. This museum is devoted to 114 years of Studebaker history and includes over seventy vehicles. For more information, visit *www.studebakermuseum.org*.

- **Walter P. Chrysler Museum:** Auburn Hills, Michigan. This museum traces the automotive age—from a DaimlerChrysler perspective. Gleaming cars, including a

1902 Rambler and a 1943 Jeep, are displayed in stunning arrangements. Also check out the gift shop. Visit *www.daimlerchrysler.com/museum* for more information.

Auto Races

The four major auto racing leagues—Formula 1, NASCAR, Indy Car, and CART—provide plenty of opportunities to see cars in action. You may also find midget races, truck races, dragster races, and other stock car races in your local area.

NASCAR

NASCAR, which stands for National Association for Stock Car Auto Racing, is the governing body for stock car racing in the United States. What makes stock cars so much fun to watch is that they're souped-up versions of four cars that you could purchase at your local car dealership: Chevrolet Monte Carlo, Dodge Intrepid, Ford Taurus, and Pontiac Grand Prix. The racing season lasts from February through November and includes locations all over the country. Get schedules and plenty of other information on the official NASCAR Web site at *www.nascar.com*.

Formula 1

Formula 1, perhaps the most well-known racing series in the world, features open-wheel cars—cars with no roofs and no fenders or any kind of metal surrounding the tires. Open-wheel cars, also called Indy cars, look very little like the car you drive to work every day. The racing season lasts from March through October, and includes stops in major cities around the world. Get the lowdown on Formula 1, including the annual racing schedule, on the FIA (Federation Internationale de L'Automobile) home page, at *www.fia.com*.

Indy Racing League (IRL)

Cars in the IRL race in open-wheel cars on oval tracks, with races heldthroughout the United States. The Indianapolis 500, of course, is always on the schedule on Memorial Day weekend. For a complete schedule and information about the IRL, go to *www.indyracingleague.com.*

Championship Auto Racing Teams (CART)

Like IRL, CART teams race in open-wheel cars, but unlike IRL, they race on both oval tracks and road courses, and they race in Mexico, Canada, Japan, the UK, and Australia in addition to the United States. The season lasts from March to November. For a schedule and lots of other information, visit *www.cart.com.*

Automotive Web Sites and Other Resources

Cool Web Sites

Finding automotive information on the Internet has changed the way Americans buy cars. Although the information isn't always 100 percent accurate, you have more information at your disposal than you can possibly use. You can find thousands of useful Web sites to use for research, as well as car shopping. The following sections provide a few sites that are most helpful at the moment. Take a look at these to see what you can expect to find online, and keep in mind that, as with everything electronic, these sites and links may change soon.

Cars.com

Cars.com is a thorough site that features useful information on a wealth of subjects—pricing guides, quotes directly from dealers on any car you choose, and a lemon check. More importantly, though, Cars.com features a link to Tom and Ray Magliozzi, also known as Click and Clack to millions of listeners of their show, *Car Talk,* heard on National Public Radio on Saturday mornings. If you want to quickly get up to speed on how to maintain and repair cars, get in the habit of listening to this hilarious call-in show. The site offers archives from the show, a Q&A section, listings of recommended repair shops, and an in-depth glossary. Visit the site at *www.cars.com.*

Edmunds.com

Edmunds.com is a one-stop shop for vehicle information, including new-car prices, auto show information, monthly payment calculator, and dealer holdback lists. In other words, this site has it all! Visit the site at *www.edmunds.com.*

New-Car Pricing and Quote Sites

Getting prices and quotes on the Web is one of the most exciting new trends in automotive sales. Armed with pricing information, you'll be well-prepared to negotiate at your local dealership. Or even better: Get a quote directly from the dealer via e-mail and decide in the privacy of your own home, under no pressure, whether you want to accept or reject the offer. You may have to drive 100 or 200 miles to get the vehicle (or pay an additional amount to have it delivered), but the savings and ease with which you can buy a car are tremendous. To get new-car prices and quotes from dealers, check out the following new-car Web sites.

- Autobytel: *www.autobytel.com*
- Autoweb: *www.autoweb.com*
- CarSmart: *www.carsmart.com*
- Kelley Blue Book: *www.kbb.com*
- Stoneage: *www.stoneage.com*
- Vehicles-on-Line: *www.vehiclesonline.com*

Used-Car Pricing Sites

Most used-car pricing sites allow you to enter not only the year, make, and model, but a host of information about standard and optional equipment and the condition of any vehicle you're searching for. You get a price range in seconds.

Note that *Kelley Blue Books* have been the used car industry standard for years, but now, instead of having to trudge to your local library to find Blue Book prices, you can find them online. It's the best place to start.

- Kelley Blue Book: *www.kbb.com*
- Auto Trader: *www.autoconnect.com*
- IntelliChoice: *www.intellichoice.com*
- N.A.D.A. appraisal guides: *www.nadaguides.com*
- Pace price guides: *www.carprice.com*

Great Auto Magazines

Even if you have no interest in cars except as transportation to and from work, car magazines—which normally include stunning photography—can be fun to read. And for the most part, subscriptions are cheap. The autumn new-car issues are worth a review even if you never thumb through the publications at any other time.

Consumer Reports

Consumer Reports is by far your best source for honest, detailed testing results for hundreds of vehicles. If *Consumer Reports* thinks your dream car has quality issues, forget that car and find another. Because they don't accept advertising dollars, the testing results are unbiased. Visit *www.consumerreports.com* to find out how to subscribe.

Automobile Magazine

This slick magazine features large glossy photos, often of luxury cars that'll make you drool. Written in a fun, easy-to-read, appeal-to-the-masses format, this magazine is like the *Tiger Beat* of car magazines. Visit *www.automobilemag.com* to start your subscription.

Automotive News

Automotive News is not a photo-based magazine with mass appeal. Instead, it's a serious weekly newspaper that's designed for industry insiders—dealers, automotive manufacturing managers, automotive suppliers, and so on—so the focus is on breaking news, the movers and shakers of the automotive world, and stock trends. The subscription is pricey, but if you want or need to follow the automotive market, it's well worth the price. Visit *www.automotivenews.com* to start your subscription.

Car and Driver

Car and Driver, the world's most-read automotive magazine, features any and all information that's relevant to new-car buyers and those continuing to drive older vehicles. It's a great resource to review before buying or leasing a car—get a copy of the new-car issue (usually available in September) before making a final decision about a purchase or lease. Visit *www.carand driver.com* to start your subscription.

Motor Trend

Motor Trend is a fun magazine to look through each month. This glossy magazine focuses, as the name suggests, on trends—what's up and coming, what's on its way out, and which concept cars will actually make it to the market. Get a copy of the annual new-car issue (usually available in September) before making a final decision about a purchase or lease, and check out their annual "Car of the Year" designation. Visit *www.motortrend.com* to start your subscription.

Road & Track

Road & Track, which bills itself as the "original automotive enthusiast magazine," is a glossy, sophisticated magazine aimed at new-car buyers and those trying to maintain their older vehicles. You'll find technical expertise and thorough road tests. Get a copy of the new-car issue (usually available in September) before making a final decision about a purchase or lease. Visit *www.roadandtrack.com* to start your subscription.

glossary

Acquisition fee: A fee that covers the cost of approving and processing your lease, which you pay when you lease a vehicle. This fee can be paid upfront or spread out over the monthly payments.

Actual cash value: The value of a used vehicle (purchase price plus any repairs) before the dealer's profit is added on.

Add-ons: Options that dealers add to cars, as opposed to options that manufacturers install on the assembly line. Examples of add-ons include CD players, truck bedliners, undercoating, and vehicle security systems.

Adjusted capitalized cost: The total lease amount, which includes all fees, but excludes any rebates, down payments, or trade-in allowances.

Amortization: The payment of an auto loan, including principal and interest. The first payments consist of nearly 100 percent interest, while the later payments will actually be paying off the principal.

Amount financed: The total amount of a vehicle loan, including the cost of the vehicle and any add-ons or options.

Annual percentage rate (APR): The annual rate of interest for a vehicle loan.

Balloon loan: A type of loan characterized by small payments for a number of years and one large payment at the end of the loan term.

Base price: The cost of the car with standard equipment and without additional options. *Also see* **Monroney sticker.**

Bedliner: A plastic coating that's fastened or sprayed over a truck bed to prevent scratches.

Blue Book: *See* **Kelley Blue Book.**

Blue Book value or price: The price listed in any of the online and paper **Kelley Blue Book** guides to pricing new and used cars.

Capitalized cost: The negotiated price of a leased vehicle. *Also see* **gross capitalized cost.**

Capitalized cost reduction: Cash payments, rebates, trade-ins, and cash back used in a lease to reduce the capitalized cost. *Also see* **capitalized cost** and **down payment.**

Captive finance company: A leasing or finance company that's associated exclusively with a particular vehicle manufacturer, such as Ford Motor Credit Company.

Closed-end lease: A lease that requires no further obligation at the end of the lease term, assuming the mileage and excess wear and tear terms have been met. However, even in a closed-end lease the lessee sometimes has to pay a disposition fee.

Collateral: Security given to offset the risk of a loan default. When financing a vehicle, the vehicle acts as the collateral, which means that the vehicle can be taken away if the loan payments aren't made.

Credit life insurance: Insurance that pays or helps pay loan balances due if the insured person becomes disabled or dies.

Cute-ute: A mini-SUV.

Dealer charges: Charges for **add-ons** installed by the dealer.

Dealer holdback: A bonus that manufacturers pay to dealers to increase their profit margins.

Dealer incentives: Money paid by manufacturers to dealers when they sell overstocked or underselling cars. Dealers can pass these incentives on to customers or keep them.

Dealer invoice: The amount the dealer pays the manufacturer for a particular vehicle.

Dealer prep: An additional charge that dealers try to impose on their customers for preparing a car for sale. The dealers are paid by the manufacturer to prepare the car for sale, so when unsuspecting customers pay this fee, the amount is pure profit for dealers.

Dealer sticker price: The **Monroney sticker price** plus options installed by the dealer.

Default: The condition that occurs when a customer doesn't repay his or her loan or make lease payments.

Deposit: Money held by a dealer until the deal closes, at which time it is either refunded or applied to the down payment. *Also see* **security deposit.**

Depreciation: The amount by which the value of a vehicle declines over time.

Destination charge: A fee for shipping the vehicle from the manufacturer to the dealer. This standard charge is available on manufacturers' Web sites and shouldn't be increased by the dealer.

Direct financing: Obtaining financing from a credit union, bank, or other financial institution instead of going through the dealer. Always check whether your dealer can beat the interest rate and other charges associated with your direct financing.

Disposition fee: A fee charged by the lessor to prepare and repair a leased car for sale on the used-car market. A lease agreement lists the disposition fee.

Down payment: A cash payment or trade-in amount from an existing car that reduces the amount of principal to be financed. A lease down payment reduces the cost of leasing the vehicle, not the cost of the vehicle price itself.

Early termination: Defined as ending a lease before the lease term ends.

Early termination fee: A penalty for terminating a lease before the end of the lease term. The lease agreement details the costs associated with an early termination fee.

Excess mileage charge: A per-mile charge on a leased vehicle for each mile over the agreed-upon amount.

Excessive wear and tear charge: A fee charged for unusual wear and tear on a leased vehicle.

Extended warranty: A contract that extends beyond the manufacturer's warranty, which may be offered by manufacturers, dealers, or after-market warranty specialists.

Factory-installed options: *See* **trim package.**

Fair market value: The worth of a vehicle at any given time.

Gap coverage: Insurance that exists for leased vehicles in which the payoff amount of the lease is paid no matter how little other insurance is carried on the vehicle.

Gross capitalized cost: The negotiated price of a leased vehicle, plus any other fees that will be paid, including insurance costs, extended warranty contracts, and so on. *Also see* **capitalized cost** and **capitalized cost reduction.**

Hybrid: A gasoline- and electric-powered car.

Insurance: Coverage in the event of a collision, theft, and so on. Many states require all drivers to carry insurance. In addition, lessors usually insist on a high level of insurance on your leased car.

Interest: Money paid to borrow money, usually expressed as a percentage per usage of time.

Invoice price: The amount the manufacturer charges the dealer, including destinations charges, but not including additional rebates and other incentives from the manufacturer.

Kelley Blue Book: The most famous car-pricing guide, now available online.

Lease: An arrangement that's similar to renting a car—the lessee can drive the vehicle but will not own it at the end of the lease term.

Lease contract or term: The agreed-upon dates of the signed lease agreement.

Lease extension: Continuing a lease after the lease term date has passed. This is similar to living in an apartment with an expired lease and simply paying your landlord every month to allow you to continue living there.

Lease-like loan: A combined lease and conventional loan. *Also see* **balloon loan.**

Lessee: The person who leases and drives a vehicle.

Lessor: The person or business who allows the lessee to drive the vehicle.

Mileage allowance or mileage limit: The total mileage the lessee can drive during the lease term without having to pay the **excess mileage charge**.

Monroney sticker: The price sticker that lists the MSRP, destination charge, and fuel economy, federally mandated to be affixed on the window of each car for sale at a dealership.

Moonroof: A sunroof.

MSRP: The manufacturer's suggested retail price.

Open-end lease: A lease that requires a payment at the end of the term to make up the difference between the projected value of the vehicle at the end of the lease term and the actual value of the vehicle.

Options: Extra features, such as a car stereo, cruise control, and mud flaps, that are installed in the car on the manufacturer's assembly line. *Also see* **trim package.**

Negative-equity financing: Financing for a new vehicle purchase that includes a payment to the finance company of the trade-in vehicle, because the trade-in vehicle was worth less than the loan balance. *Also see* **upside-down loan.**

Options: *See* **add-ons.**

Port-installed options: *See* **trim package.**

Purchase option: The option to purchase a leased vehicle at the end of the lease term.

Purchase option fee: A fee to purchase a leased vehicle at the end of the lease term.

Realized value: The value of a vehicle at the end of a lease term.

Rebate: A payment made by the manufacturer directly to the consumer. A rebate can be used as a down payment.

Residual value: The projected value of the vehicle at the end of the lease term.**Security deposit:** A refundable deposit on a leased car, generally equal to one or two monthly payments, that ensures the lessee will abide by the terms of the lease contract.

Soft roader: A combination SUV and station wagon.

Sport-cute: A mini-SUV.

Sticker price: The base price plus manufacturer-installed options, destination charge, and fuel economy. *Also see* **Monroney sticker.**

Sublease: Allowing a sublessee to take over payments on a lease. This is usually not allowed in lease contracts.

Subvented lease: A lease that's partially subsidized by the manufacturer or dealer and thus offers lower monthly payments.

Term: The length of the loan or lease, usually measured in months, not years.

Title: Written evidence that proves the right of ownership of a specific vehicle.

Title fee: Fee paid to search for the title.

Trade-in value: The amount the dealer will pay you to buy your existing car to use as a down payment on a new car.

Trim package: Several options bundled together and costing less than the individually priced options added together.

Up-front costs: Payments made when signing the lease agreement. These costs may include the first month's payment, down payment, a refundable security deposit, taxes, vehicle registration, and so on.

Upside-down loan: When the value of a car is less than the balance due on the loan.

VIN (vehicle identification number): A number assigned to the vehicle by the manufacturer that also appears on the vehicle's registration and title. You can track stolen cars by their VINs.

Walk-away lease: *See* **closed-end lease**.

Warranty: A promise from a dealer or manufacturer that if a vehicle has a problem within the warranty period, the dealer will repair the problem at no charge.

index

The ⦿fastread Series

An affordable series that provides a quick-fix for immediate questions, *fastread*® is the solution for those of us who don't have all day. With its straightforward, get-to-the-point style and accessible organization, you get the facts you need to know—in no time flat!

1-58062-508-8
$5.95 (Canada $8.95)

1-58062-696-3
$5.95 (Canada $9.95)

1-58062-530-4
$5.95 (Canada $8.95)

1-58062-509-6
$5.95 (Canada $8.95)

1-58062-511-8
$5.95 (Canada $8.95)

1-58062-393-X
$5.95 (Canada $8.95)

1-58062-510-X
$5.95 (Canada $8.95)

1-58062-697-1
$5.95 (Canada $9.95)

Get *fastread*®, get the information, and get on with your life!